W9-BTL-921

ALSO BY DAVE ITZKOFF

Lads: A Memoir of Manhood

COCAINE'S SON

COCAINE'S SON

A MEMOIR

Dave Itzkoff

VILLARD  NEW YORK

Published in the United States by Villard Books, an imprint of The Random House Publishing Group, a division of Random House, Inc., New York.

VILLARD BOOKS and VILLARD & "V" CIRCLED Design are registered trademarks of Random House, Inc.

This work is based on an article originally published in *New York* magazine on July 24, 2005.

Grateful acknowledgment is made to Ice Nine Publishing Company for permission to reprint an excerpt from the lyrics to "Dupree's Diamond Blues" by Robert Hunter, copyright © Ice Nine Publishing Company. Used with permission of Ice Nine Publishing Company.

Library of Congress Cataloging-in-Publication Data
Itzkoff, Dave.
Cocaine's son: a memoir / Dave Itzkoff.
p. cm.
ISBN 978-1-4000-6572-1 (hbk.)—ISBN 978-0-345-52439-3 (ebook)
1. Itzkoff, Dave.   2. Cocaine abuse—United States.   3. Children of drug addicts—United States—Biography.   4. Drug addicts—Family relationships—United States.   5. Fathers and sons—United States—Biography.   I. Title.
HV5810.I89 2011
362.29'84092—dc22   2010040501
[B]

Printed in the United States of America on acid-free paper

www.villard.com

1 2 3 4 5 6 7 8 9

First Edition

Book design by Caroline Cunningham

For my mother,

who kept us together

When I was just a little young boy

Papa said, "Son, you'll never get far

I'll tell you the reason if you want to know

'Cause child of mine, there isn't really very far to go"

—ROBERT HUNTER

COCAINE'S SON

CHAPTER 1

He was such an elusive and transient figure that for the first eight years of my life I seem to have believed my father was the product of my imagination. The adult world that I traveled through was populated almost exclusively by women: there were the teachers who trained me on the multiplication tables, the state capitals, and the three branches of government; their aides and assistants; the babysitters, nannies, and housecleaners; the plastic-gloved, hairnetted cafeteria workers who called me Pepito as they ladled out my hot lunches; the school nurse who schemed to deplete me of my saliva with her tasteless wooden tongue depressors; and a jumpsuit-clad handywoman named Celie who spent fruitless hours wading through the school trash to find the loose tooth I threw away, fearing its escape from my mouth meant I was falling apart. There was my sister, who came into existence two years after me; a pair of fragile but living grandmothers, sundry aunts, great-aunts, and cousins. And there was Mom, who sat above them all on this pyramidal structure of progesterone. But there was only one Dad, or so I was told.

It required the combined energies of these many women to discharge the duties normally provided to me by the indefatigable and infinitely resourceful Mom; each had her specialized skills and knowledge, but Mom equaled, encompassed, and surpassed them all. By day, she was not only the Chooser of Clothes, the Maker of Breakfast and the Conveyor to and from School, the Holder of Hands and the Kisser of Cuts and Bruises. She was the Giver of Language, who provided names for the distinctive vagrants who wandered our block—Rudolph, with his bright red nose, and Froggy, whose raspy voice carried all the way up from the gutter to our twenty-fifth-story apartment on East Fortieth Street, with what was then an unobstructed view of the East River—and the Tutor of Numbers, who showed me how the digits of Manhattan's streets grew bigger from south to north and from east to west. She taught me that the person whom others called Maddy but whom I knew as Mom were one and the same, and she reminded me that there was another person named Gerry whom I knew as Dad, and that Mom and Dad each had a mom and a dad, too.

By night, she tirelessly rubbed her cool, foul-smelling jellies into my chest when it was filled with phlegm, operated the dials of a mysterious hissing device called the vaporizer, and massaged my feet when the pain from their bones, growing and stretching without my consent, caused me to cry. At dawn, she rose again to implore me not to be frightened by the apocalyptic rumblings of the newspaper trucks roaring forth to make their morning deliveries, backfiring like pistols as they went.

She was my co-conspirator when I sought extra sick days to stay home and watch game shows; she was my chief defender when, as she observed me on my first attempt to purchase my own food at McDonald's, I was pushed out of line by a grown-up female customer. ("I told her she was very rude," my mother explained, and for a time I believed this was the most devastating thing a person could be called.) And when she did not feel like dealing with the world, she was my date to a thousand matinees, to movies for which we would always arrive late and then stay in our seats and watch a second time so we could see them in their entirety. Many years passed before I learned that a movie could be watched just once at a theater.

All she asked in return was that I abide, to the letter, by a byzantine system of laws, regulations, and taboos known only to her and forever in flux. Don't play Spider-Man on the weblike netting that extends over the side of our terrace and into the inviting blue sky. Don't leave the dinner table until you've taken five more bites of your food—so determined because I was five years old, and the following year the penalty would go up to six bites. "Hand, hand, fingers, thumb!" she would call out when we approached the edge of the sidewalk, requesting that we lock digits before she escorted me across the street. Sometimes she would stand with me at a distance from the curb, watching the cars whiz by as the traffic sign changed from WALK to DON'T WALK and back. And sometimes, when the sign would blink its final DON'T WALK warning, she would get an excited gleam in her eye and clutch my tiny fingers forcefully and exclaim "Let's go!" and we would race off into the intersection, always making it to the other side just in time.

There was something melancholy about her rules, their preoccupation with the manifold ways that I could be injured and their foreboding certainty that I would be lost the moment she took her eyes off me or a situation arose that she hadn't prepared me for. Even her rules of thumb for shopping at the neighborhood supermarket were a little sad. "Don't ever get attached to anything here," she would say. "The minute you start liking it, they replace it with something else."

When she really wanted to feel sad, she turned to the hi-fi we kept in our living room. Digging deep into the milk crates she used to house the family record collection, she flipped past the cheerful *Sesame Street* soundtracks she had accumulated for me and my sister, and a well-worn copy of *Free to Be . . . You and Me* that promised a new country of green fields and shining seas; past the psychedelic copy of *Sgt. Pepper's Lonely Hearts Club Band,* with its construction-paper insert of a fake mustache and epaulets that I was not allowed to cut into even though the page clearly said CUT HERE; past the Bette Midler albums and the cast recording of *A Chorus Line,* with their exotic descriptions of adult activities and hilarious, forbidden words like "tits" and "ass," until she stopped at a record by a fuzzy-haired young singer named Janis Ian called *Between the Lines.*

Tucked far away in my bedroom, I could hear the soft guitar bossa nova of the title song, and through the walls I could just about make out the lyrics, about desperation and Friday-night charades, and high school girls with clear-skinned smiles who married young and then retired, and a quietly chilling refrain about what it means to learn the truth. I knew my numbers well enough to count how many years it would be until I reached that apparently terrible age of seventeen, and how many had elapsed since my mother had been that old. But I could no more imagine what I would think or feel then, or how she thought or felt, than I could comprehend how adults put on their jackets all by themselves without laying them upside down on the floor in front of them. I had watched school years come and go, and the seasons transition from winter to summer to winter again, but I hadn't been on the planet long enough to know that when things changed, sometimes they didn't change back.

What I could understand about the song was that my mother appeared to have less in common with the awkward girls lamented in its lyrics—ravaged faces, lacking in the social graces—than with the beauty queens its singer coolly set herself apart from. I knew, to look at her, that my mother was beautiful, and I knew it long before Sigmund Freud told me to think that. If I looked around our apartment, I could see that its other male tenant, wherever he was, had turned it into a shrine to her, filling it with framed photographs from every era that he knew her: a trophy from some long-ago fishing trip, as he stood with one arm around a giant marlin and the other around her, her sun-dappled skin wrapped tightly in a bikini; a goofy relic from a costume party when she wore a rented wedding dress and he wore a T-shirt meant to look like a tuxedo. They did not yet have me in their lives, and still, somehow, they were happy.

In the camphor-scented residences of my grandparents, I had seen the most tangible and luminescent tribute to her divinity: the tear sheet from an old modeling campaign she had done for Johnson & Johnson shampoo, in which she was asked to do no more than tilt her head to one side and hold a brush to the shimmering oscillations of hair that flowed in jet-black waves from her head. Her carefree manner in those pictures seemed utterly incompatible with the stifled sobs that accompanied her Janis Ian listening sessions. What could someone so pretty be unhappy about?

Long after my mother had put me and my sister to bed, when the sirens had stopped screaming and our darkened apartment was filled with only the murmur of our refrigerator and the occasional rasp from Froggy down below, he would come home. I would hear him first at the front door, the metallic tinkling of steel against steel as a key wandered its way into the lock and turned the tumblers, then the sighing of floorboards giving in to his weight as he lurched and lumbered from room to room, shuffling from the foyer to the living room and stopping at my bedroom door. A trembling hand would tousle my hair, and an ample body would wrap his arms and legs around me and envelop me in its warmth, so close that I could feel his stubble against my own bare cheek and a warm tickle ran up my neck each time he exhaled. He took rapid, erratic gulps of air, and he would say to me, "Davey, are you up? Can I talk to you?"

"Hi, Dad," I would answer.

I would listen as he would talk, and talk and talk, about whatever was on his mind. One topic usually prevailed. "You know, David," he said, removing his glasses from his beaky nose so I could see the sincerity in his wide, round eyes, "don't you know that sex between a man and a woman is the most beautiful and natural thing there is? It's okay to want it. It's okay to want it from a woman. You've got to let them know that you want it. That's how God made the game. But He knew that He couldn't make the game too easy, right? Or else where would be the challenge? Do you know that it took me years to figure this out? For years I suffered—oh! how I suffered!—when girls would reject me. Do you know that your mother is the first woman who didn't turn me down? She showed me that it was beautiful and wonderful. I don't ever want you to be scared. I don't ever want you to suffer like I suffered."

Less frequently, he would tell a recurring story about his father. "Do you know, David," he told me on many occasions, "I was once rummaging around in the glove compartment of his car and found a glass eye? And I knew it was his, but for so long, I was too scared to tell him. Finally, one day I got up the courage to tell him, and I said, 'Dad, I know you wear a glass eye, and I want you to know I don't think any less of you.' And do you know what he said? He said, 'Gerry, if it hadn't of been for that glass eye, I could have been president.' And I hugged him and I kissed him"—by now he was shivering and choking on his own tears—"and I said, 'Dad, you always could have.' "

Sometimes he wanted to pass on bits of philosophy and wisdom he had picked up in his travels, whose usefulness he knew I would not grasp right away. "You know that when somebody dies," he would say, "they aren't really gone, right? As long as we keep them in our hearts and remember them, they live on forever, don't they?"

When his lesson had ended, my father would prostrate himself on the surface created by my and my sister's adjoining beds, and he would fall asleep, snoring loudly. Eventually, I would drift off, too, and when I woke up in the morning, he would be gone, leaving me to wonder if I'd dreamed it all.

Just as I believed that everyone lived as we did, in bustling, overcrowded metropolises, surrounded by bums and decaying brownstones and high-rise apartment complexes that stretched into the clouds; and that everyone went to a private school and was transported there each day by a private van that picked him up and dropped him off at his front door; and that everyone was Jewish to the extent that we were Jewish and knew who was *not* Jewish because they not only exchanged gifts on Christmas but also went to church, or because they were black, I believed that all families operated as ours did. There was a mother whose job it was to do all the household chores, to cook and clean and raise the children and give them their Oreos before bed, and there was a father who did whatever he did, at whatever hours he did it, and was thus entitled never to be questioned about it.

Somehow I knew that I was the only boy whose father confided in him as mine did, who trusted his son so completely and had such faith in his intellect and maturity that he would make it his mission to prepare his offspring, aged five or six or seven, for these stark grown-up lessons in sex and death and missing eyes. Meanwhile, all my peers would have to wait to discover these things when an indifferent world and callous experience forced the lessons upon them. Separated though we were by some thirty-seven years, I thought my father saw in me an equal and a second self. I thought I had a special friend.

Unlike any other person I had known so far, my special friend was not the same man at all times of day. There was the exuberant, affectionate husband and father who referred to the marital bed he shared with my mother as the "Our Bed," a reminder that my sister and I were always welcome in it, too. He had no shortage of diminutives for me, either: in his lexicon, I was the Ace; I was his Pal; I was the Wild Man; I was the Edge Man, so called for my preference for sitting at the farthest, most dangerous precipice of the Our Bed; I was Pizza Head, for the time I fell noggin-first into a pizza he and my mother were eating on the Our Bed.

I was the Chicken Man, who had his own theme song, set to the tune of the Beatles' "Nowhere Man":

He's a real Chicken Man
And he comes from Chicken Land

Another nickname he gave me, Chicken Itzy, was so pervasive and so deeply embedded in my consciousness that when I first encountered the Mayan ruins of Chichen Itza in a middle-school history textbook, I had to stop and wonder if my father had built those pyramids there and named them after me.

This father was so endlessly attentive with me, so imitative and appreciative of anything I did or said, that when one of my enunciations amused him, it forever became a family catchphrase. "Out de door!" he would say when he left the apartment for the day, just as I did, or "Hat on!," meaning it was time to pack up one's things and go. Using his own special made-up vocabulary, he would call out the scrunched-up facial expression I made when I got sleepy ("The kid's got mouse eyes!") or the way my hair stood on end when I first woke up ("The kid's got pull-'ems!"). Until I learned to pronounce the word correctly, he referred to his spectacles as his "guh-lasses," and when I would reach up and try to grab them off his nose, he would playfully warn me, "Guh-lasses are *not* a toy." When I succeeded and his glasses went spilling to the floor and I knew I'd been bad, he would make an exaggerated grimace and sing me a silly song to calm me down:

Big trouble
Big bad trouble

He was not always absent from my life. He could be counted on for at least an occasional appearance at crucial events, to watch me at the second-grade pageant as I stood in a toga made from bedsheets, behind a podium wrapped in construction paper and decorated with the legend s.p.q.r. spelled out in gold and purple glitter, and recited from memory Marc Antony's funeral oration from *Julius Caesar*. Later, that same man would emerge from the back of the school gymnasium to give me a congratulatory bear hug, his rumpled clothing hanging off him like dead leaves and his breath so pungent that it arrived at my nostrils long before he leaned in to bestow upon me a congratulatory kiss.

Some days he would come home brimming with energy and

wanting to take me to the neighborhood tropical-fish store, where he would wander the aisles for what felt like hours and chat up the salesmen about the largest tanks they sold and the latest innovations in water-filtration technology, while I sat on the floor and stared at the fish, wondering if they knew that I appreciated how it felt to be confined in a tiny box all day, and wishing that I could be for one moment that toy diver blowing bubbles from inside his colossal diving suit.

One night my father returned to our apartment and decided then and there that he was going to drive from New York to the home of a business client who lived far north in the Adirondacks, near the Canadian border. I decided that I wanted to go with him, because I knew it would get me out of school, and he allowed me to go, unfazed by my mother's disapproving scowls. On a pitch-black winter's night, we rode up I-87 together for hours, not in my mother's dilapidated Lincoln Continental that got only AM radio and was always breaking down on the way to Hebrew school, but in my father's pristine BMW, in which the leather seats always smelled vaguely of carsickness. We were two intrepid explorers, castaways with nothing between us except an open road and a single cassette of a whiny, adenoidal troubadour singing of knights in armor and silver spaceships and only love can break your heart and ominous intonations of what's going to happen when the morning comes. Twice I fell asleep and twice I woke up just in time to watch my father lose control of the car on slippery patches of ice as we spun out into banks of snow. After the second wipeout, the car could no longer drive forward, and for only a couple of miles did my father insist that he was going to complete the trip driving in reverse. A tow truck provided us with our ride home.

What did he do to keep me in a steady supply of Dr. Seuss books and videogame cartridges, to pay for my private school and his BMW and his tricked-out fish tanks? Nothing glamorous and nothing different from exactly what his father had done and his father's father before that: he sold fur. Not the coats but the skins themselves, torn from the bodies of coyotes and foxes, beavers and minks and lynxes, turned inside out or pounded flat, treated, and preserved. He did not perform those tasks himself; he bought the pelts in small or large quantities, waited for markets to shift, and then sold them to other traders at a profit. To do this required that he go to a storefront every day and handle the skins, inspect the merchandise when it came in, and present it to others that might buy it from him. When he returned home, he reeked of flannel and denim and the musky oils that dripped from these hides, and of something else. I have smelled many unbearable odors since, and learned to distinguish the difference between the smells of tons of discarded food left to fester in the sun; vomit that has crystallized on the sidewalk; and men on subway trains soaked in their own urine. Still, I have never figured out what that additional scent was.

The fur industry of my grandfather's age had thrived to where it was the equal, in size and prestige, of the garment district it bordered on Manhattan's West Side. But by the time of my childhood, it was sequestered—so fate ordained—to a few dilapidated buildings in the shadow of Madison Square Garden. On the days I was brought to my father's office, I would walk hand in hand with my mother past an off-track-betting station, a couple of parking lots, several gray and cheerless edifices where various unknown trades were conducted, finally to a building with a large, wide window that bore the legend GERALD ITZKOFF FUR MERCHANT (and a smaller window that, for the sake of nostalgia and superstition, still read BOB ITZKOFF & SON).

My visits here consisted of waiting for several hours while my father finished his workday. I listened to him screaming over the phone at his clients and his rivals; screaming at the day workers who did the manual labor, retrieving the fur from storage and tying it up in bales; and screaming at my mother, who had recently begun to help him with the bookkeeping. Here, he was a different man from the one who sat at our breakfast table, armed with a thousand running jokes that equated going to work with committing suicide, who from nowhere would quote Edward G. Robinson's mournful death rattle from *Little Caesar*—"Mother of mercy, is this the end of Rico?"—and who responded to my mother's demands that he get in the shower already by miming a noose being drawn around his neck. Here, he was not the same person who had become so fixated on a short, poetic proverb, possibly of his own invention, about the meaninglessness and futility of all life's efforts—"Nothing means nothing"—that he would sometimes recite it under his breath without even realizing he'd said it.

Here, he was dynamic, aggressive, competitive. He wanted no one else to win except the people he was partnered with, and those who rivaled him he wanted to see utterly vanquished. He made it no secret in all his telephone calls around the office, and the ones that followed him home late at night, and his monologues in which he would talk himself through his plans of attack and profess his invincibility, often ending with him declaring: "We're gonna get 'em, do you hear me? We're *gonna get 'em*."

I wandered the cold concrete building, peeling large, jagged flakes of paint off the surfaces as I went, bounding up and down precarious metal staircases made slippery by decades of musky, gunky buildup, hiding among the burlap bales that towered over me in the refrigeration units, drawing on walls already decorated by the retinue of employees who had worked here for months or weeks before they disappeared with their wages.

Sometimes on my explorations, I would open up a cabinet or a panel and find the decomposing bodies of dead rats. Other times I would reach into a drawer and discover magazines, reminiscent of those he kept hidden around the apartment, with crinkled, yellowing pages populated by photographs of radiant, naked women whose ready poses and unfamiliar anatomies stirred strangely pleasant sensations in corresponding and similarly untested parts of my body. Often these pictures would be embellished with great dollops of purple and orange matter, the encrusted remains of what I intuitively knew was my father's blood. I could glance only briefly at these tableaus before being overcome by a humbling feeling that I was gazing at something sacred, an admixture of the distillated essence of my father and a little bit of me that, when combined with the holy vessels depicted in those photographs, held the secret to creation itself.

It was around this time that I went through a phase when similar urges made me want to reach out and grab for my mother's breasts, and my father became my great protector when I needed him to shield me from her sudden ferocious retaliation. It was not just my unknowing molestations that set her off; her fury would follow when I hadn't obeyed one of the rules she had explicitly set forth, or when I transgressed an invisible boundary she had forgotten to convey to me. Maybe I'd neglected to wash my hands and face after coming home from an afternoon spent scavenging the trash cans for Oscar the Grouch; maybe I'd sat backward in my seat at the dinner table, just to see what would happen if I did it, or maybe I'd pulled my knit cap over my face in protest when I refused to watch the St. Patrick's Day parade after she'd fought her way through the Fifth Avenue crowds to get me a good look at the procession.

The openhanded blows would come swiftly across my face, sometimes just a single bolt of lightning, sometimes a flurry of hailstones. Once I'd absorbed that first stinging swipe, the rest landed numbly with no impact. But sometimes my father would be there to catch her by the wrist before a single slap had landed, so her own momentum would send her falling backward. Sometimes he wouldn't be there at all and the blows would keep coming and coming, and I'd stare at the front door of our apartment, hoping that at any moment it would be thrown open by my father, who would swoop in, his forearms extended and bulging like a comic-book character's, and rescue me.

But who could protect us when he was the one we needed defending from?

In the same way I believed our happy family was alike to all other happy families, I extrapolated that every coupling of a mother and a father must have some regularly scheduled moment, most often on a late Saturday afternoon, after the father has spent the morning snoring a hollow, staccato snore able to drown out the traffic, the bums, and the Con Edison plant below, when the parents will initiate a titanic argument in which walls will be rattled, doors will be slammed, and fragile household artifacts will be shattered. This was all normal, I thought, and an obligatory part of adulthood, that the mother cries and locks herself in the bathroom, and the father kicks at the door, shatters the mirror on its other side, and in an effort to coax her out, hurls the ceramic pumpkin in which his wife saves her quarters for the laundry machine.

In my family, such fights persisted until my mother screamed and called my father a junkie, a funny-sounding sort of word that reminded me of her broken-down Lincoln. A few minutes later, my father would storm into my room, the collar of his undershirt stretched halfway to his waist, possibly with scratches across his face, and wearily instruct me: "Look at me. Look at what your mother did to me."

This must be what happens in every family, I assumed, *because it is what happens in mine.*

It must happen as surely as those unpredictable and out-of-nowhere instances when my father was home at midafternoon on a weekend or even on a weekday, tottering around the apartment like a bear that had come out of hibernation, when he'd lose his temper because my videogames were too loud or I'd asked for his help with my fractions or my Roman-history crossword puzzle and I couldn't remember that "governor" was the title both Americans and Romans gave to the person in charge of an entire state.

"You *know* this one," my father would insist.

"No, I don't!" I'd shout petulantly.

"*Yes,* you *do,*" he would hiss back with menace in his eyes.

I'd laugh and call him the silly word I had just heard my mother use: "You're a junkie," I'd say, because past observation had taught me that it was an instant victory. It was the one rebuke for which he possessed no comebacks.

His eyes would fill with fire, and his hot breath would emanate from his flaring nostrils as he grabbed me by the wrist. "What did you just call me?" he would shout. "Do you even *know* what that word *means?*"

Next he would storm out of the room and seek my mother. "Do you hear this, Maddy?" he would shout at her. "You hear the way he talks to me? Where do you think he gets it, huh? From *me?* From his *private school*? Well, let me tell you, there'll be no more of *that*. No more private school for him—he is *out*. Out of *school,* out of *here,* out on the *street,* for all I care!"

"Stop it, Gerry! Stop it!" she would shout back at him. This would be followed by the sound of his bare, heavy feet trammeling across the floor, and he would reappear in my room in nothing more than his underwear and grab me by the arm.

"You hear me?" he'd shout. "You're *out of here.*" He'd open our front door and deposit me in the hallway, slamming the door shut as he hobbled back inside.

Eventually, my mother would come out and retrieve me. But what was I supposed to think until then? Should I have concluded that this was an act intended to remind me that beneath his docile exterior, he possessed power and was capable of taking things away from me at any moment? Or should I have prepared to gather up my belongings in a bindle and make my way from town to town, shining shoes and painting picket fences as I went? These people, my parents, had taught me how to speak and what to think and what to fear, that turtles die if they aren't fed regularly and that you can't just walk down the street saying "Hi, man!" to every person you see. How was I supposed to know when they weren't being fully honest with me?

Back when the question of who I should call my best friend seemed like the most crucial dilemma I would face, I granted that title to a boy named Justin. He was identical to me in many ways: we were both small in stature—"shrimpy," I believe was the term at the time—both phenomenally fond of videogames, even when they consisted of crude monochrome blips that bobbed up and down on the TV screen, and both had fathers who never seemed to be around the house (although his father, I knew, had a much cooler occupation than mine: he was a dentist, *and* he owned a liquor store).

The most important function Justin served was keeping me company through Hebrew school, a tedious obligation that had somehow insinuated itself into my life without my agreeing to it or asking for it. The rigors of attending a regular school five days a week were demanding enough; in first grade, after I left one school building, I would travel to another, where I was told, after having spent my entire life up to that point memorizing and mastering the only alphabet I assumed existed, that there was a second one I was responsible for learning.

Before I enrolled at Hebrew school, and even before I started at private school, my preschool and kindergarten education came from classes offered by an extremely liberal, extremely Reform synagogue in midtown Manhattan. There, any pedagogy about Jewish faith or history was doled out gently, mixed in with the grape juice and finger paints, nap hours and folk-guitar sing-alongs. The depictions of the fabled, far-off land of Israel that were occasionally presented to us had no relation to the world I inhabited—why did everyone appear to live on barren, heat-drenched farms like the planet Tatooine of *Star Wars*, and why were they always in need of our money to plant trees? The legendary heroes whose exploits we were told of hardly seemed heroic at all, always doing exactly what they were told by God, even when His orders were utterly inscrutable.

There were only two exceptions to this rule. One was my namesake, the biblical David, who proved that the most lopsided height differential could be overcome with a single act of epic violence. The other was Judah Maccabee, who spent eleven months of the year boxed away and forgotten, to be trotted out in that month when the secular department stores began to hang their

Christmas decorations, to remind us of days long ago when men, much different from the kinds I knew and the kind I was sure I would grow into, took up swords and shields to drive out their oppressors and reclaim what was theirs. This was my favorite time of year, and not just because it entitled me to a king's ransom in presents. To my mind, the Hanukkah miracle was not that some hoary lamp burned for eight days on a single day's worth of oil, but that there were Jews who, for once, had stood up for themselves and won.

For unspecified motives, my parents sent me to Hebrew school at a Conservative temple, and this was the reason for all my troubles. We had never set foot in a synagogue as a family, and yet once a week I was donning a yarmulke to sit next to Justin in a classroom that was smaller and shabbier, and whose students were twitchier and nastier, than private school had prepared us for. There, the congregation's rabbi, a rotund and cheerful but ultimately stern man who called everyone by Hebrew name, taught us the subtle differences between the jagged letters *vav* and *zayin,* the imposing, ax-handled *dalet* and its tailless cousin *resh*. His weekly lessons came from a pair of well-worn paperback workbooks that, no matter how inviting their cartoon illustrations of men gardening and farming and women cooking and cleaning might be, we were not to doodle upon or we would have to pay for them at the end of the year. Coinciding with the start of the regular school term, our Hebrew-school calendar began with the harvest feast of Sukkot and the alien fruits used in its celebration, the husky, unappetizing *lulav* and the lumpy, malformed *etrog*. Within a couple of weeks, we had moved on to the high holidays and the traditional ritual of being shamed by one's rabbi for not attending temple regularly.

My difficulties were compounded when I graduated to second grade. My attendance was doubled to twice a week, and the responsibility for my education was handed off to the rabbi's wife, the first of many instructors I would meet who savored the license that the occupation provided to constantly tell children they were wrong. My classmates were the same distracted, unengaged malcontents with whom Justin and I had sat through first grade, and who, in a year's time, had still not learned to distinguish among the serrated, angular Hebrew characters that hung like faceless portraits from the classroom walls. The lesson plan from the previous year—Sukkot, Rosh Hashanah, Yom Kippur, endless guilt—was repeated without variation, only this term we were let in on a great and terrible secret: everything we had been taught about Hebrew was a fraud, because the written language used no vowels. This was not the last time that my discovery that an essential historical fact about Judaism had been withheld from me would make me very, very angry.

In the meantime, Justin and I had each other to keep sane and share that window of time in the afternoon after regular school ended but before we were shipped off to the gulag. On one typical appointed Hebrew-school day, we were in my apartment, playing videogames and awaiting my mother's return from work so we could be transported to our fate. However, the door to my parents' bedroom was shut tight, which meant my father was home and fast asleep. I silently decided that this was the day I was going to make my stand.

The telltale clicking and clacking of a key in our front door announced my mother's arrival. In a singsong voice, she said, "It's time for Hebrew schoolie," which was about as tantalizing as it could be made to sound.

Justin dutifully put down his game controller and began gathering his belongings. But I didn't look away from the screen. "No," I said.

"David," my mother said, becoming stern. "Don't make me turn off this TV set." After a moment she did so anyway.

"No," I repeated. "I don't want to go to Hebrew school today." Justin looked perplexed. Had I miscalculated that Hebrew school was as irritating to him as it was to me? Or had he never seen anyone talk back to his parents?

My mother took my two Hebrew-school workbooks from a living room shelf and brandished them like weapons. "You're going to Hebrew school, and that's final," she said.

But how could I tell her that it wasn't final? How could I articulate to her that the teacher was mean and the kids were idiots, that I got yelled at no matter what I did even when I knew I was the best in the class, and that deep down I suspected the more vehemently and dogmatically someone tries to instruct you in something, the less likely it is to be true, and besides, I'd rather spend the time playing more videogames?

"I don't want to go to Hebrew school today," I said as forcefully as I could, which meant as loud as I could. *"Now or ever."*

From deep within the apartment, another doorknob turned, followed by a pair of heavy footsteps erratically but deliberately heading our way. My gambit had worked. The father had been roused.

He was, as usual, in his underwear, his hair was scattered in every direction, and his eyes were half shut. But to me, he was my Jewish hero: my biblical David, my Judah Maccabee, the rebellious protector of my faith.

"What's going on, Maddy?" he murmured to my mother.

"Tell him," she said. "Tell him he has to go to Hebrew school."

"Well," he said wearily, "does he want to go to Hebrew school?"

I answered, "I don't want to go to Hebrew school."

"So if he doesn't want to go," my father said, "why are you making him go?"

"Because, Gerry, he has to learn that when he makes a commitment to something, he has to see it through. He won't listen to me, but he will listen to you." She sounded exasperated.

"If he doesn't want to do it for himself," my father fired back, "you're not going to be able to make him do it. So just let him stay home." His voice was booming now. Justin was crying, and I was beginning to realize that maybe not everyone's family operated like mine did.

"Uh-uh," my mother said, raising her voice to match my father's. "You're not letting him out of this. He has to go whether he likes it or not." She started waving the Hebrew schoolbooks at him, like she had at me.

Suddenly, he grabbed the books out of her hand. "Oh yeah?" he said, and in one continuous movement, he made his way from the living room to our terrace and swung open its sliding door. "If I say he doesn't have to go," he shouted, *"then he doesn't have to go!"* He took one step onto the terrace and flung the books over the side like Frisbees.

I raced to the terrace myself, to see if I could catch a glimpse of the books as they twirled and spiraled to the ground, but they had already fallen out of sight. I was beaming. Justin was bawling. My mother was fuming. I stayed home with my father. My mother took Justin to Hebrew school.

I stopped going to Hebrew school, and as I ascended from second grade to third grade, I became renowned around the apartment for my performance as Charles Darwin in the Dalton School's production of *The Great Naturalists,* in which I sang a climactic tribute to the discovery of evolution called "Strange, How Things Change." But I could tell that things were not all right in the household.

The gaps between my father's appearances had grown to two

and then three days. My mother was around plenty, filling ash-trays and half-empty coffee cups with stubbed-out cigarette butts, scribbling lengthy notes to herself on yellow legal pads that she would hastily pull to her chest whenever I tried to glance at them, and sneaking into the bathroom with the telephone, its curlicued cord stretched taut across the living room as she tried without much success to talk in secret.

One afternoon I returned home from a day blissfully free of Hebrew school to hear the sinister strains of Janis Ian's "At Seventeen" already wafting from behind the door. When I let myself into the apartment, my mother was waiting for me, sitting cross-legged on the couch, dead cigarettes strewn around her like ashen confetti and her makeup smeared by tears, as she clutched one of those notepads from which she began to recite a monologue she did not trust herself to deliver without cue cards.

"This is something your father and I have been going through for a long time," she said without looking up from her notes. "We have tried and tried, but I don't see how it's going to work out. We want you to know that we both love you very much."

This obtuseness was too much for an eight-year-old. "What, what is it?" I impatiently asked.

Finally, my mother looked up at me. "Your father and I are getting divorced," she said.

I started crying, though I'd known the announcement of my parents' divorce was a rite of passage I'd someday have to undergo—something that happened to all my classmates, like getting the chicken pox or expanding your apartment into the one next door to yours.

"But why, Mom?" I wanted to know.

"He's a drug addict, Davey," she said. "He's been addicted to cocaine almost your whole life."

The information still wasn't computing. Hadn't my parents seen the public service announcements that played round the clock on our televisions? Didn't he understand he could just say no? Didn't she realize that an honest, thoughtful conversation would sort out the problem? "Why does he take drugs?" I asked her.

"How should I know?" she snapped back. "If I knew that, maybe I'd be on drugs myself." This was not a reassuring answer.

I started to think about what life was going to be like from now on. There would be fewer incidents that would set off my mother's temper, perhaps, and no special protector to defend me when they occurred. Maybe my mother would start dating again, even remarry, and we'd all be driving down Park Avenue in our new family car when we'd look over at one of the grassy dividers and see my father camped out among the bushes, surrounded by his few remaining possessions and his clothes ripped to shreds.

"Can I still live with Dad?" I asked my mother. The quavering look in her eyes told me this wouldn't be possible.

I realized that everything was over. No more family, no more Mom, no more Dad. No more videogames, no more action figures, no more visits from Justin. I thought about that confrontation between my parents a few months ago, and I wondered what would have happened if, instead of tossing my Hebrew schoolbooks off the balcony, my father had hurled me over its side? Would I have plunged to the ground before anyone could take notice of me? Or could I have willed myself to resist the tug of gravity and floated up into the sky?

CHAPTER 2

For all the strange and shocking circumstances that had nearly brought our family to the brink of collapse, stranger and more shocking still was what happened next: nothing. Every afternoon I came home from school expecting to find my mother waiting in the living room with all our belongings packed into suitcases, ready to hit the road. Every time she introduced me to a man who seemed to be roughly my father's age, I wondered, *Will this be the person who replaces him, takes us in, and gives us a new home?* But the divorce that she vowed to extract from my father never came. With each morning that we woke up in the only apartment I had ever known as my home, my dread of an impending cataclysm subsided a little more, until the day my mother pulled me aside and told me, "Look, your father and I aren't getting divorced anymore, so there's nothing for you to be nervous about. You can stop wetting your bed now."

There came a later day when I thought my father was going to dismiss the possibility of our family's dissolution once and for all. Though he had been weakened and diminished by the recent upheaval and absent from the scene even more frequently than usual, he summoned the strength just once to gather us all—his wife, his son, and his daughter—around the dining room table to deliver what he told us was a crucial announcement. My sister and I leaned in close as we listened for what would surely be the formal declaration that our parents' hostilities had concluded. "Do you know," our father began with purpose and intensity, "that your mother and I haven't had sex in over a month?" We children made noises of revulsion as we sprang from our seats and fled the room.

Now I knew everything about my father, I thought. When he went missing for days, I knew what he was up to. And when we arrived home at the same time, crowded into an elevator with a few unsuspecting neighbors, and he'd put his hand on my shoulder and say in a soft, ragged voice, "When we get upstairs, I want to talk to you about something," I knew enough to tell him, "I don't want to."

He would answer, "But *I* want to."

The elevator doors would shut, and I would look at the man I once thought was my special protector, his chest heaving, his eyes bloodshot and bulging, his body reeking. I would look around at the faces of the bystanders temporarily trapped with us, trying to catch their gazes before they darted their eyes away, and I would think: *Now who is going to save me from this?*

Sometimes I would find him on the street, pacing, like he'd remembered how to get himself all the way back to where he lived but couldn't recall how to walk through the front door. I would recognize him at a distance, and as I drew closer to him, he would be unable to look me in the eye, let alone focus on anything.

"Dad," I would ask, "what are you doing out here?"

"David?" he would answer. "Is that you? Come here, I want to talk to you about something."

I could feel the heat of his breath wilting my skin, and see the rivulets of mucus that he made no effort to stem as they dribbled from his nostrils and meandered across his mouth. Even in these moments I couldn't tell that anything was wrong with him.

I would compliantly follow him to wherever he led me, to sit on a nearby bench or to deposit ourselves on the curb, and I would listen as he recited a familiar lecture. "David," he'd say, "don't you know that sex with a woman is the most beautiful and wonderful thing there is? But you can't be afraid of it, like I was. And you can't be afraid of rejection, either. Because it wounded me, David—oh, how it *wounded* me. It made me scared, small. But I can make sure that doesn't happen to you. You can benefit from my errors. You know that if you ever wanted me to get someone to do it with you, I would pay for that, right?"

When he'd trail off in midsentence or forget what he'd been talking about, he would bury his face beneath the sleeve of his jacket like a vampire shielding himself from the sun, or insert his nose directly into the breast pocket of his shirt and take a huge and audible sniff.

That was when I would shake off my denial and accept what was going on. "Dad," I said with revulsion, "you're getting high right now, aren't you?"

Though he had been caught, he was too sheepish to admit the truth. So he stared at the ground, pretending he hadn't heard me, shuffled his feet, and took another snort.

For months I had been priming myself for total, catastrophic change, attuning my senses to their highest degrees of receptiveness, raising my defenses to their highest levels of readiness, but the upheaval I expected did not occur. The war games I had been running in my mind were a waste of psychic energy, and now I could not dial back my state of readiness. I was misreading signs, leaping at false alarms and failing to anticipate when authentic, drastic change was headed my way.

Left on my own, I began to develop strange habits. I became fixated on syllables—the number of syllables in words, in sentences, in passages of text I read, and in song lyrics I heard. I began counting them out in my head at first (12), then started counting them silently on my fingers (26), flipping my digits up and down as I went (37). Sentences or phrases that contained multiples of five syllables were the best (20), because then they completed a hand—all my fingers would be up or down when I reached the end (45). If they contained too few or too many syllables (13), then I would try to think of words that could be added to them (29) to make them come out even (36). Do you see now (40)?

In addition to my unique neuroses, another, more universal stirring was beginning to make itself known. It seemed to wash over me all at once, around the age of eleven or twelve, the promiscuous, paranoid suspicion that everyone everywhere around me was fucking: not only the stripped bare, fully exposed females in my father's hidden magazines, who left me obsessed with the possibility that under the right circumstances, a woman's clothes might fall entirely off her body, but the disobedient frat boys and the compliant co-eds they chased in the movies I saw; and the impossibly suave bachelors and the backtalking babes they flirted with on the television shows I watched; and the superheroes and heroines, in the comic books I read, whose every bulge, curve, and ripple was perpetually threatening to burst forth from their skintight costumes; and yes, on rare occasions, my parents.

Before I realized it, the boys I rode with in a private van to a private school went from fantasizing about action figures, fast cars, and baseball cards to strategizing about the girls in our class, who had gone the furthest, and just what they'd do to them, in precise and elaborate detail, if they ever had the chance to get them alone. Their knowledge astounded me and their aggression frightened me. How could I compete with them, and what would any girl want from me, with my contrary anatomy, my frantic fingers, and my uncooperative bladder? What was I supposed to do to make them take notice of me, and what was I supposed to do with that attention when I at last received it? When I got visual confirmation of the answer one life-altering night, at a fateful all-boys' slumber party at Chris Dworkin's house, from a most peculiar videotape that Alan Perlmutter produced from a brown paper bag, I was invigorated and horrified by the act that awaited in my future.

I had never received a proper education in these affairs. All I had were the results of my repeated experiments in rubbing myself against my bedsheets, and the sound in my head of a man's voice telling me that sex was a beautiful and wonderful sacrament and I should never live my life in fear of it or in fear of having it denied to me. But why did I have to be told this was even a possibility? Would I have been so fearful if I'd never known it was something to be afraid of?

My first school-age crush arrived in third grade. Her name was Courtney Kolesnikov, and she was a girl with sleepy purple doe eyes and a sleek Roman nose who had already started growing to statuesque heights while all the boys were still underdeveloped and—what's that word again?—shrimpy. She was delivered to me one night in a dream, in which I imagined that some invisible ghost was trying to pull down the pants of all the girls at school; hers were the only ones that this unseen phantom successfully removed. I reflected on this the next morning, and by the end of the day I realized what it meant: I liked a girl.

For weeks I kept the secret, dreading that I had committed a crime and would soon be found out for it. But I did not do an effective job of hiding my feelings from her or from my classmates: at every opportunity, I had been sitting next to her during math and reading sections, running alongside her as we did our laps in gym class, surreptitiously slipping her my unwanted Archie and Richie Rich comics. What I had admitted to myself with great difficulty was easy enough for other students to codify into a taunt: "David *likes* Courtney." They said it to me with spite and derision, turning a word that I thought conveyed endearment and affection into an act of loathsomeness, and they hung it around my neck like a millstone. They chanted it when I was tagged out in softball, when I gave the wrong answer to a multiplication problem or couldn't find a seat on the bus, and especially whenever I came anywhere near Courtney—or any other girl, for that matter. Soon Courtney herself became convinced of the wrongness of my feelings: if, in an act of classroom charity, I tried to offer her the answer to a teacher's question, she rolled her eyes in disdain, and if I tried to run alongside her in gym, she just pumped those long legs harder and sped off. She despised me for liking her, and I hated myself for it.

This went on for almost two years, until fifth grade, when she stopped me on our way out of the classroom. "I have something for you," she said, reaching into her backpack and producing a small envelope that she handed to me. She turned around and walked away before I could open it.

The envelope contained a very literal love note: a piece of paper on which she'd drawn a musical clef and two notes with our initials, D.I. and C.K., inside them, sitting happily side by side. I had no idea what prompted her change of heart; maybe my months of silent, slavish devotion had worn her down. I was so excited by the news that I slipped the note into my backpack, told no one about it, and did nothing.

More weeks went by before I called Courtney and asked her on our first date. On a day of parent-teacher conferences when we were off from school and no one there would know we were out together, I took her, unsupervised by adults, to an afternoon matinee of *Raising Arizona,* an early Coen brothers comedy that mightily challenged our middle-school minds. The mood, more panicked than romantic, was not enhanced by a ticket taker who asked if we were brother and sister; I made absolutely no physical advances on her during the afternoon. We politely said goodbye after the thoroughly perplexing film. I called her that evening to make sure she had gotten home safely.

It was our last date. The more I thought about the tremendous burden this romance represented, the more it scared me. I was repulsed when I thought about myself and couldn't bear to involve her in this disgusting fraud. I looked at my little boy's hands and saw the lethal claws of a carnivorous beast.

Courtney started calling to ask why I wasn't calling her. I never had a good answer. "Don't worry," I told her, "I still like you."

In our last phone conversation, she sounded like she was going to cry. "Why did you do this," she asked, "if you never really liked me?" I hung up because it was easier to run away. I went into my backpack and retrieved the love note, now creased and beaten from perpetual agitation, pocked by the pencils and uncapped pens it had been tossed among in my carelessness, and put it in the trash. When Courtney and I saw each other in classes or around the halls, we had a sensible reason for avoiding eye contact and keeping our interactions to an awkward minimum. And that's how my cowardice ruined my first relationship.

After devoting many months to reconciling and rekindling their marriage, my parents decided their next project was to find a new home, a tidy suburban baptismal where they could wash away the frustrations and distress the city had imposed on them. From the answering-machine messages left by their real estate broker that I kept surreptitiously deleting, I learned that they had bought a house in northern New City, a locality that had attracted them not with a name that promised freshness and a new start but with the Ford dealership where they bought their first SUV. I had never seen the town, but as soon as I finished ninth grade, I would have to live there.

The verdict on my future arrived at a frustrating time, just as I was getting acclimated to the workloads that awaited me and the caste system that had built itself around me in my first year of high school; just as my spring-term position as the assistant manager of the girls' softball team was getting me out of gym and into the company of several very tall, very strong young women; just as my nose decided it was going to grow away from my face as fast as it could and see if the rest of my body could keep up with it. The transition was social suicide, and I told none of my classmates or teachers that I wouldn't be returning in the fall, savoring the shock and dismay I imagined they would feel when my absence occurred to them early the following September.

Somewhere on a yellow bus ride to my first day at a public school that I could have visited over the summer but petulantly chose not to, I remembered the other half of that equation: you don't get to attend your own funeral, don't get to hear your mourners lament your loss or wish aloud that they'd gotten to better know the scrawny smart kid who was terrible at dodgeball and terrific at Super Mario Bros., and at some point everybody moves on. A new smart kid easily ascends to fill the void, and a new assistant manager for the girls' softball team is as easily recruited.

In the short term, our family's relocation seemed to help control my father's drug problem. Now, at least for the hours of the day when he and my mother were angrily commuting back and forth to his Manhattan office, he had no opportunity to fuel his habit and no access to the people who supplied him or enabled him, the sullen faces and dingy, dimly lit places that encouraged him to cap off his grueling slog with a tasty, intoxicating line.

Our new home, with its alien enormity, had another unanticipated effect on our clan. While we lived in the city, we had been confined to an apartment that, though larger than any place I have since resided, made it impossible for us to go about our days without at least crossing paths in the hallway. The new dwelling offered a multitude of passages, escape routes, and personal chambers—a private bedroom for each of us, a surfeit of rooms to slip into at the sound of another person's approaching footsteps—and we took advantage of them. We ate our meals at different times of day and retreated to our rooms quickly, while the big-screen television my father had purchased for the living room rattled the corridors with news of the Rodney King riots, the attempted-murder trial of Amy Fisher, and the failed reelection campaign of George H. W. Bush. Had you seen this house from the road or driven past it by accident at any hour of the evening, you would have had no idea it was occupied by people, let alone people who knew and loved one another, let alone a family.

My only respite from this tedious routine were the weekends, when there was so little to do around the house and so little to watch on television that my father would turn to me and ask, "Do you want to learn how to drive?" We'd pile into his sedan or the SUV whose purchase was the first link in the chain that shackled us to the suburbs, and he would drive me out to the emptied high-school parking lot or a deserted end of a shopping center, perpetual reminders of my captivity, transformed into the training grounds for my escape.

As a teacher, my father had an unprecedented ability to memorialize and recall my errors of the past: his greatest concern was that I not repeat a mistake I made when I was ten years old and allowed for the first time to sit on his lap while he sat in the driver's seat and I accidentally steered the car into the tiniest of fender benders; he made me practice jamming on the brakes over and over until he was confident that I would do the same in a real-life panic situation. But once he allowed me to let the car gain some momentum, my father was also a remarkably patient tutor, who showed me repeatedly how the car handled differently when it was shifted in reverse and I was looking through the rear windshield, until I understood it as inherently as he did. If I drove too fast, his only instruction to me was to silently depress his palm, as if pushing down a column of air, and if I scraped the car against some stationary object, he would only look at me and grimace, as if to say, *Don't do that again*.

He never fully explained why it was so important that I become a proficient driver as quickly as possible; he never needed to. In his prouder moments, he would say things like "Do you know you're already a better driver than your mother? She's been driving for thirty years, and she'll never understand it like you do." In a moment of sudden forlornness, he would confess to me that when he was growing up, he never had a car of his own, and he vowed not to repeat that mistake in raising me. "As soon as you get your license," he would say, "I'll take you to the dealership and

you can pick out any new car you want." On one condition: "Just
don't drive into the city until I first show you how to handle it."
What did I care about that particular restriction so long as I had
the ability to leave this town in any other direction and never return?

There was one occasion not too long after when he asked me to
violate his self-imposed taboo. It was a Saturday, the kind of day
on which my father might otherwise be furthering my automotive
education if he were around. But I hadn't seen or spoken to him
since the previous day. He called me that afternoon.

"David," he said in a voice that was thin and shaky, like radio
static. "I'm in the city. I need you to come and get me."

"Oh God," I said. "You went and got high, didn't you?"

He was ashamed, as always, but not too ashamed this time to
admit it. "Yes," he answered.

"I can't believe you," I told him. "You make all this progress,
and then you just throw it away. You're right back at square one,
do you realize that?"

No reply.

Though I would have loved nothing more, at age fifteen, to get
behind the wheel of a car without a license and drive all the way
into the city, and to have told anyone who might have tried to im-
pede my mission that I was doing it on my father's incontrovert-
ible orders, I answered him in spite: "I'm not coming to pick you
up. You figure out how to get home."

It would have suited me fine if my father never returned to the
house. But by that same afternoon he was back, transported by a
Good Samaritan who had found him on the streets of Manhattan
and who, miraculously, drove him all the way back to New City
without promise of reward or remuneration when my father, no
less miraculously, was able to remember the directions back to

his house under the influence of cocaine. He went straight to his bed and fell fast asleep. His mysterious benefactor phoned our house for three straight days to make sure he was all right, until he finally took the hint from the unanswered messages and stopped calling.

In the meantime, I was woken early the next morning by my father, who was already out of bed and crashing hard after his previous day's intoxication, lecturing my mother loudly on a subject that I soon deduced was me.

"You have raised an awful, *awful* child, Maddy," he hollered. "Who treats a person in need that way? You wouldn't treat a *dog* that way. You don't kick a dog when he's down. Well, let me tell you something, Maddy, he is *done* in this family. Finished! He is *cut off* from now on. I'm not giving him anything, and I don't want your mother helping him out, either. He is not to receive one cent from her. Not *one red cent!*"

I wondered if he realized that I could hear him through the whole horrible oration, the stomp of every angry word as it made its way up the stairs, forced itself past my bedroom door, and into my ears. Did he know that this particular lesson was having as much an impact on me as his many months of driving instruction? Did he know that as I heard him, even as I was motionless and wrapped underneath my bedcovers, I was vowing to myself to never again be put in a position where I would have to depend on my father for anything? In any case, our irate promises, both spoken and unsaid, did not remain intact for very long.

At my new school, I had a teacher in a late-period class who did not observe the traditional adult custom of ignoring how the fickle hands of puberty had molded my nose into an elongated and misshaped form: he who used to call me "protractor." It might even have been a nickname I came up with and told him he could call me because it was easier to take than any of the other titles he'd given me. On an evening in the fall of my first term, my mother and father were introduced to him at a parent-teacher night—some harmless little ritual that my parents came home from in tears.

I was sitting at the computer playing videogames when my father approached me and fell to his knees.

"David," he said with great trepidation, "have you ever wanted to do anything—you know—about—you know—your nose?"

"What do you mean, Dad?" I knew what he meant, of course, but I wanted to know what had finally compelled him to ask me about it now.

"There was this one teacher tonight," he said, and I immediately knew which one he meant. "He really likes you, he thinks you're just a terrific student. And he sat me and your mother down, and he said, 'I want you to know I think David's a great kid. He's adjusting fine so far. He's doing well in class and starting to make some friends. Now all he needs is a nose job.'

"David," he continued, "if your mother and I paid for it, would you—you know—want to get one?"

I knew my adolescence had made me ugly, and now that I knew my parents knew it also, there was no point in denying myself the remedy that would correct it. In a rite of passage as familiar as any bar mitzvah, I waited out the rest of the school year so I could have my nose job at the start of the summer, putting off the road test that would earn me my driver's license to instead spend several days convalescing, drinking orange juice and laughing at pictures of Ringo Starr, whom I no longer resembled.

Before my junior year of high school, I had picked out an event as my coming-out party, the debut of the new me and my emergence into properly adjusted teenagerdom. My new face had secured me an invitation to a summer party by a girl in my social studies class named Ellen Greenfield, a skinny, sweet little princess with long raven hair and the tiniest of bumps in her nose. (My theory at the time, confirmed by later events, was that she was conducting research for a future plastic-surgery procedure of her own.) The party was a no-parents-allowed affair that her parents were paying for, at a restaurant that was within groping distance of the suburban purgatory I had been confined to all these months, whose remote location had never done me any good until now.

I thought I would finally get to be brave, the way I'd always imagined I could be brave. If I could envision myself as a confident person, without constantly calculating the pitfalls, without being perpetually distracted by visions of the ways in which things could go wrong—if I didn't even know that events could turn out otherwise, I could will them to be so. I could see myself being the center of attention at the festivities, the subject of a newfound curiosity—a curiosity that I would parlay into admiration, which I would then use to get Ellen all alone, win her over with my resurgent confidence, and then—and then—well, I wasn't sure what was supposed to happen next. All I needed to set this plan in action was a ride to the party.

That same summer, my father became embroiled in a feud with my mother's side of the family. Her father, my grandfather, had suffered a terrible fall and broken his hip, and this time it wasn't a fall he was going to recover from. My grandmother was too old and infirm to take care of him, and there was no clear consensus about what should be done with him. My mother and grandmother were leaning toward moving him into a nursing home; my father was strongly opposed. He became so consumed with my grandfather's fate that he could not find the time to bring himself to work because he was in a perpetual state of argument with my grandmother. From anywhere in the house, I could hear the muffled sounds from my parents' bedroom of his feverish telephone debates with an enfeebled woman believed to be at least eighty years old and who sometimes mixed up the names of her own children.

"Let him die with dignity," he was urging her, as if my grandfather's fate were already preordained. "Let him die at home."

What did I care? I had a party to get to. Even better, I had the guarantee that someone would be on hand to chauffeur me to and from the event.

It was the day of the party. I was dressed up in my nicest jeans and my cleanest T-shirt. I had spent many minutes at the bathroom mirror, eyeing my new nose from every possible angle to make sure the old one wasn't growing back and convincing myself I could really do this. I waited for the furor of my father's most recent battle with my grandmother to subside, so I could let him know it was time for him to ferry me to my momentous event.

He was sitting on his side of the bed he shared with my mother, still dressed in the undergarments he wore to sleep the night before and probably for several days previously, staring down at his feet as if performing arithmetic on his toes, and breathing slowly.

"Dad, come on, it's time to go," I reminded him.

He answered as if talking in his sleep. "Okay," he said. "Just give me a minute."

I waited, wandered the house, gazed upon my nose a couple more times in the mirror, then reentered the room. He was sitting right where I had left him, no more clothed than the last time I saw him.

"Come *on*," I whined. "I've got to get to the *party*."

I stood over him while he applied his pants to his legs, like he was spreading a resistant lump of peanut butter over an endless terrain of bread. He put his arms through his shirtsleeves, slipped a single button through whichever buttonhole he could find, and called it done. He started fumbling around for his car keys.

"Are they in your pants?" I asked him.

"Oh yeah," he said.

"Don't you need your glasses?" I added.

"Right."

I bounded down the stairs and to the door, telling my father to follow me when he stopped on the landing and seemed to forget where he was supposed to be going. I buckled myself into my car seat and prepared for adventure.

It took me a while to notice that there was something strange about the way my father was driving. He was ambling along the local streets at a cautious, imperceptible pace instead of hurtling through them at maximum velocity. And his precise control of the vehicle was not in evidence; he steered the car as if it were a boat, wobbling side to side on an inexact trajectory. Though we had the road to ourselves, he sometimes slowed down as if another car were in front of him; I had to remind him to keep his foot on the gas pedal to keep the car moving.

He was making a right turn off the local road and onto a four-lane highway when, without warning, he missed the turn almost entirely. He took it too wide, ending up in the oncoming lane with the flow of traffic pointed at us, a red traffic light the only barrier that stood between us, them, and a head-on collision.

"Jesus Christ, Dad, what the hell are you doing?" I screamed. He had enough sense to navigate the car to the shoulder, still pointed in the wrong direction, before the oncoming traffic was upon us.

Once I was sure we were out of danger, I looked at my father. With the engine still running and the car still in gear, his head was slumped on his chest. He struggled to keep his eyes open.

"Dad," I said, "you're high right now, aren't you?"

"Yes," he answered.

"Come on," I said. "Out of the car." I extracted him from his seat and helped deposit him in mine, then took his place behind the wheel.

I thought about the freedom and power I possessed in my two hands. I could still drive myself to the party, leaving my father to hopefully fall asleep in the car and not drive himself away and kill himself in a separate, successful accident. I could drive us back into the city, back where maybe things weren't perfect but where I was at least happy, where nothing this awful had ever happened to us. Or I could take off for parts unknown with my father by my side, the two of us winding our way through America like Ryan and Tatum O'Neal in some modern-day update of *Paper Moon*. If I sped away with him, what state would my father and I end up in before anyone realized we were missing?

What I heard, when I allowed these impulses to run their course, was the first stirrings of a voice within me that had spent many months practicing its lines in private and now, though it was not quite ready for a performance, was sufficiently prepared to give a convincing rehearsal. It told me, *Be responsible! Be an adult! Do what you think a man would do in this situation! Even if you've never seen an example of what a man does! Invent one for yourself! Follow that person's lead! Whoever he is!* It was a quiet voice, but it spoke with conviction. It led me all the way back to the house, where I helped my father into bed and he fell fast asleep.

I felt I had to call Ellen and explain to her why I wouldn't be at her party. I didn't want her to think I was one more insensitive, adolescent jerk who was always begging off important social commitments with preposterous excuses. I reached her at the restaurant, where it sounded like the parent-free festivities were already under way. But I couldn't seem to summon the voice.

"My dad is a drug addict," I blurted out to her, the first time I'd revealed this to anyone outside my family. "He's been one my whole life. He always lets me down right when I need him the most."

"Whatever," she said. And that's how my candor ruined what could have been my second relationship.

I took my road test a few weeks later and failed it. When I took a retest a few weeks after that, I failed that, too.

CHAPTER 3

College loomed on my horizon like an amusement park, a massive Ferris wheel that presented me with a new and tantalizing opportunity in every car as it whirled and turned. It promised academic excellence, impeccable faculty, and bountiful resources to conduct my studies. It vowed a student body composed of young strivers all equally committed to their scholastic pursuits, to challenging one another's potentials and to furthering one another's goals, and a bucolic campus securely tucked away from the corrupting influences of authority figures and parents. It pledged access to a fresh pool of brave and experimental female colleagues, unaware of my previous reputation and facial features and open to myriad forms of sexual congress the likes of which I had only read about in the letters columns of the magazines in the farthest reaches of my father's closet.

College called out to me like a carnival barker, coming on to me with its well-honed and irresistible sales pitch, declaring that it was everything I hoped for. Anything I wanted it would find for me, and anything I wanted it to be it would become. Once I walked through its gates, it promised I could shed my previous identity and construct a new one according to my wishes. It guaranteed me that the arena I was about to enter, and each one following, would be a perfect meritocracy, where I would be judged solely on my ability to perform a task and my will to see it done. Here was a world where whatever I had been before didn't matter—all that was important was what I wanted to be. *Put aside all previous shames and abandon all embarrassments,* it whispered. College assured me that it was the path between me and my ideal self, and it swore to me that the desire to travel this route was all I needed to complete the journey.

College was a liar.

I arrived on the campus of Princeton University at the end of the summer of 1994, delivered there one August morning by my uncharacteristically and antiseptically quiet parents. Of all the schools I had applied to and been accepted into, from Dartmouth to the University of Southern California, Princeton turned out by accident to be the closest to us geographically: it was only a two-hour drive of undifferentiated New York and New Jersey highways, a straight southward shot past outlet malls and shopping centers until one hard right turn took you past the soccer, lacrosse, and rugby fields, the mansions of the upper-class eating clubs and the Center for Jewish Life, and then you were there, on its chockablock campus of Gothic quadrangles, Ionic-style Greek temples, one Frank Gehry–designed library, and a rusty Henry Moore sculpture. The change in scenery was abrupt, and the minimal road trip afforded no time to adjust.

Aside from a family visit we had made to Princeton almost a year earlier, back when I had no idea what I wanted in a college other than for it to be different from high school and far, far away from it, my parents had largely kept themselves out of my college application process, never asking to review essays or standing over me to make sure my submission materials were mailed out on time. My father, in particular, had committed himself to a superstitious vow of silence, refusing to put his thumb on the scale even by encouraging me to consider certain schools or by offering his opinions of the ones I had applied to; he was afraid his slightest attempt to influence my opinion could have traumatic and unintended consequences down the line. What if he made it clear he favored one school over another and I didn't get in? What if I chose to attend a university based on his preference and I later discovered I disliked it? What if he told me not to go somewhere and I went there anyway to spite him? What if his actions in any way led to his disappointing his son? Wouldn't it be better, then, not to act at all?

On this day of all days, I expected my father to be teeming with paternal advice, eager to guide my transition and take advantage of this last opportunity—for the next four years, at least, and possibly forever—when he would be the sagest, most seasoned adult male in my sphere of influence. If nothing else, I thought I would hear the final iterations of one or perhaps two stories he had lately been recounting to me from his personal experience, stories that were his personal favorites because they were germane to my situation and because I was old enough to hear them; because they seemed to offer general life lessons without suggesting specific courses of action that could later be contradicted or proved fallacious; and because no story in our family gets told only once.

The first story told of my father's own attempt at attending college—the first time he dropped out of school, not to be confused with the second time he bailed on his bachelor's degree. In

1956, at the advanced age of sixteen, he enrolled at Tulane University in New Orleans, where one of his very first lectures was in a calculus class taught by an instructor named Dr. Goto. As my father and his fellow students took their seats, Dr. Goto, a small Japanese man with a three-piece suit and a briefcase, was working his way from one end of the classroom to the other, filling every square inch of chalkboard space with inscrutable formulae made even more cryptic by his cramped handwriting. Any hope that the lack of clarity in the professor's printed expression would be compensated for by a lucid and mellifluous oratorical style were quickly dispelled when Dr. Goto, who, in the years following World War II and the Korean War, had come to teach calculus to American students in the Deep South, began speaking at ninety miles an hour about *"Ze fukshun!"* and *"Ze dewivative!"* In especially animated tellings of this story, my father might exclaim *"Ze fukshun! Ze fukshun!"* a few more times and add, "Nobody knew what the fuck he was talking about."

At that moment, my father said, "You shoulda seen all the kids that picked up their textbooks and made a beeline for the door." He, however, was not one of the students savvy enough to exit the class. He stuck out the semester, and for his efforts, he was rewarded with a failing grade, the first of several unsubtle nudges that would eventually prod him out of school before his freshman year was completed.

That was one tale he had been telling me a lot lately. This was the other: as a teenager growing up in the Bronx, my father once traveled from his home turf in Pelham Parkway to neighboring Parkchester, where he and a friend climbed to the roof of the friend's apartment building to eat fried chicken and to smoke pot. After getting high, the boys began to get silly, and their loud antics and the chicken bones they were hurling to the streets below aroused the suspicion of the building's tenants, who called the police and had the boys arrested.

The story did not end with the punitive ear-twisting that my father received from his mother when she bailed him out of jail.

When my father was summoned before the draft board some years later, all that the army knew of him was his name, his age, and his arrest record, which showed he had been busted for marijuana possession, so they naturally assumed the worst about him. "We employ some of the best doctors in the nation," the army told him. "We could help you kick your drug habit for good."

"I'm sorry," he answered, probably stifling a grin, "but I'm a hopeless addict."

For as much as I knew of my father's drug history then, this was easily my favorite story about it, and the more I have learned about him since, the more enamored of it I have become. No one in the story gets hurt, and it's kind of funny, though the joke is funnier if you know its true punch line, that my father really did grow up to become addicted to a far more harmful substance. Also, it seemed to offer an embryonic display of the verbal craftiness that would serve him well in later life. For all I knew, the incident may have been the only thing that kept my father from being conscripted and killed in one of our nation's earlier ill-considered wars of choice—which would mean that I owe my existence to my father's drug use.

The moral of his first story was clear: *If this was the best I could do,* my father seemed to be saying, *just think how low the bar has been set for you, my son. Look at how little you need to accomplish in order to surpass me.* If I simply showed up for my first lecture, I was already my father's equal. If I completed a single course with a passing grade, I was his hero. And if, after four years, I returned to that man—the onetime genius who had graduated from high school two years early only to flunk out of college in under one year—with my own bachelor's degree from an Ivy League institution, I was his king.

The point of my father's second story was more ambiguous. He wasn't strictly saying that he gave me his permission to take drugs; oh, no, the part of his life that overlapped with the entirety of mine had been one long argument against that. And though he loved to spend his summers in a cabin upstate in Monticello, New York, fishing in the morning and watching FOX News in the evenings, I don't think he was advocating a libertarian worldview that one should always seek to undermine authority and misrepresent oneself to government agencies.

No, I think the lesson he hoped this legend would teach me was a more general one: that it was okay to try new things and important not to be afraid of them; that it was permissible, even necessary, to make mistakes, get silly, throw chicken bones off rooftops; that it was only through the acquisition of experience— no matter how awkward or self-thwarting it might be—that a boy becomes a man. Experience cranked the engine of time, and on occasion time transformed our humiliating defeats into minor victories.

This was what he had been telling me repeatedly, incessantly, until the day he and my mother conveyed me to the location where my trajectory departed from theirs, depositing me at the mysterious machine whose inner mechanisms would be known only to me but from which their vantage point appeared like a great black box working its unknown effects on their son to alter him into something different and unfamiliar, and they suddenly went mute. Unlike the other sets of parents we saw that day, who chaperoned their children with grace and appropriate distance, my mother and father did not take their cues to depart as soon as they saw I had been delivered safely with all of my belongings; they continued to hover and rotate around me like satellites until I told them they could leave. I unlocked the door to my ancient dormitory, saw its brick walls decorated with green oxidized stars to memorialize the occupants who had died in world wars, and felt a stuffy, humid draft begin to creep in through the stone flue.

I was idealistic enough those first few weeks to believe that any other freshman would be as unfamiliar as I was with the school and its structure and that any new person I encountered could be converted into a friend through conversation. But there is a way that two people look at each other when they meet, even passing strangers whose glances align for an instant. In that moment, their eyes can convey warmth and kindness, indifference or re-vulsion, calculated and communicated in a fraction of a second. When I looked at my new classmates, I thought I was putting out a message of curiosity and openness, but I must have been commu-nicating desperation and vulnerability, because what I saw di-rected back at me was ambition, aggression, and antipathy. My college tenure would be spent vying to maintain my averageness against an infinite number of competitors with an infinite range of skills developed from an infinite number of backgrounds, and it would be a losing battle. They came from their country clubs and cotillions, conservatories and community-service projects, preparatory schools and magnet programs, with preexisting con-nections and private instructors, old friends who came with them to school and more than sufficient charisma to make new ones. I showed up with four Beatles CDs and the same Janis Joplin poster that had hung on my wall in high school.

So for a time I fell in with my three roommates, who all wanted the same thing I did and, who like me, had been led to believe by urban legend and John Hughes movies that by simply being in a place where lots of women also happened to be and behaving as we normally would, gravitational forces would naturally draw them to us. But over the months and semesters, after many Saturday nights spent scanning the dog-eared freshman facebooks we had dutifully purchased on our move-in day, poring over the female faces and wondering what the bodies attached to them might look like, and renting every movie from every library on campus and watching it in the solitude of our cold and drafty den, we had not made much progress. We began to go our separate ways: one roommate found his peers in an a cappella singing group, and a second was absorbed by his friends in the school orchestra; the third never quite got his act together and trolled the dormitory halls telling our female neighbors things like "You know, I've never watched a woman put on her makeup before."

That left only me, and it meant that down the mean streets would have to go a young man who was not himself mean. I knew where the women would be, and to get to them I would have to get myself to the parties, fraternity and sorority houses, keggers, mixers, dimly lit dormitories, and back-alley taprooms that sat just outside the jurisdiction of campus police. There, I felt, I was certain to find women—women who wanted to be with actual men who looked like they strode right out of baseball cards and deodorant ads, instead of hairless, prepubescent cherubs from Raphael paintings with tiny corkscrew penises. There, I believed, this same youthful innocent who had not yet consumed an entire can of beer would be corrupted into ingesting much more illicit substances. It was paralyzing to think about, and it was all I thought about. I was trapped inside my mind, and my mind was the only place I allowed myself to live.

They were extraordinary, the false realities that I could invent, the elaborate fantasies that I could concoct from the thinnest of circumstances, and they became more delirious and desperate when some actual women came into my social circle. There was the little Jewish girl with the short chestnut hair and almond eyes whom I met on an off-campus hiking trip, whom I circled and circled but could never bring myself to dive in on. There was the coed, only heard on the phone and never seen, who was set up with me at random for a campus-wide computer-dating dance, for whom I bought an unasked-for bouquet and made an unsolicited dinner reservation, and whose distaste and bewilderment I completely understood when she called to back out of the whole arrangement at the eleventh hour. There was the tall and flaxen-haired roommate of a friend of a friend whom I was too scared to make a move on when I walked her home from a party one night, but whose cafeteria meals I was perfectly at ease crashing and whose dorm-room door I was completely comfortable standing outside at any time of day or night, whether she was home or not. The little Jewish girl with the short chestnut hair and almond eyes even came back to me a second time, ready to let me take another shot at whatever she had to offer, but all I had learned in that time was how to sit actionless in intimidated awe of her, and she drifted away again.

That was just my freshman year.

As a sophomore, I continued to fantasize about the graduate students for whom I checked out books at the art-library desk where I worked, and phoning up girls who said they already had boyfriends at other schools, until I befriended a young woman who lived on my hallway. After a few weeks of hanging out, doing homework in my dormitory living room, and sitting at the back of a chartered bus, swapping swigs from a hidden bottle of Goldschläger on the way to an R.E.M. concert, I had concluded in my messed-up, desperate noggin that we were in the midst of a relationship that was on the verge of getting physical at any moment. That lasted until she started telling me about the dreamy junior she had her eye on, at which point I viciously and abruptly broke up with her in my mind. I wrote savage eviscerations of her in my journal, fixated on rueful Bob Dylan songs, copying out the lyrics to "Idiot Wind" over and over on my binder in silent dedication to the latest unrequited crush to spurn my unarticulated advances, certain this music by a twice-divorced journeyman who'd known everyone from Woody Guthrie to Federico Fellini had been created to address the personal and specific needs of a nineteen-year-old virgin who'd lived his whole life between New York and Princeton.

I vowed to call her out on her perceived callousness, and when I never made good on this threat, I swore never to speak to her again or even explain how it was that she had offended me. I wondered then, as I do now, if she had the slightest sense of the turmoil she was wreaking in my life. Did some fraction of my agony ever get through to her, and did any part of it remain after I cut myself off from her? Or was she one more woman who wandered blissfully through the world, another unknowing assassin who killed men, like me from afar without ever having to see the crime scenes?

It was the midpoint of my sophomore year, and I had found a means of distracting myself from solitude, a medium that offered me access to the part of my brain that didn't know how big the world was and how tiny and inadequate I had become, something I could turn to at any time of day when I wasn't feeling the way I wanted to feel or when I didn't want to feel anything at all, and that was drugs.

I started growing my hair long, traded my glasses for contact lenses, and ditched the remnants of my high school wardrobe for

CBGB T-shirts, in tribute to my Manhattan homestead, and a silver chain I wore around my neck with a padlock I had attached, in honor of the first-wave British punks I had recently discovered. These superficial changes eventually drew me into a whole new group of friends who worked at the college radio station and had memberships at the alternative eating clubs and dining co-ops; who turned me on to all the indie rock and classic rock I had missed in my time spent playing my four Beatles records over and over again; who looked and dressed like Willie Nelson in the 1970s, disheveled and intimidating from afar but utterly harmless up close.

From the fateful night when I was handed a bong for the first time and, not knowing how to approach the apparatus, tried to fit it inside my mouth and asked if they made them any smaller, I became a different person. In those moments when everyone else at a party started shooting stealthy glances at one another and then disappeared to parts unknown, I was no longer the guy left behind to wonder where all his buddies had gone. I was a part of that group, who got to visit the shabby, half-lit rooms where all the action went down, always littered with unwashed clothes and half-eaten sandwiches and smelling vaguely of cats even when no cats were present. I got to watch the rituals, in which an acolyte would retreat to a corner and turn on a stereo softly playing *American Beauty* or *Pretzel Logic,* and a high priest would sit at the edge of a bed or stand over a dresser drawer arranging his relics and manipulating his paraphernalia, packing a bowl of marijuana so compactly and precisely that it looked like a newly mowed field in miniature. Then he would offer up the first hit to whoever looked like he was most in need of relaxation, and eventually, we'd all take a hit, and another and another and another and another, and we were happy and content to share the same air and smoke and saliva. If you overdid it one night and couldn't make your way back to your bedroom, you fell asleep right where you were on the floor, woke up the next morning, and wandered home in a delighted daze.

Having concluded my prepared statement, I'm ready to take your questions.

Did I, as a direct result of my new drug-consuming identity, meet any women who, in their blissed-out state, found me more attractive or were willing to sacrifice a small bit of their dignity in exchange for access to, among other things, my stash? No.

Did this identity give me enough of an edge to make me sufficiently beddable to a couple of girls who would have paid me no notice in my button-down days? Probably.

Did I, as the son of an addict, who had seen firsthand the havoc that drug use could inflict on a user and his loved ones, have any hesitation about taking those first steps along a route that could lead me to the same cul-de-sac where my father resided at length? Didn't I hear in the back of my head an endless echo of that vintage 1980s television public service announcement in which the guy barges in on his kid doing some unidentified substance and demands to know where the kid got it, and the kid answers, "From *you*, all right? I learned it by watching you," and then a Deeply Serious narrator comes on and says, "Parents who use drugs have children who use drugs"? Are you fucking kidding me?

How do I think my father would have felt if he could have seen me in these moments?

I'm not going to say that he gave me his permission to behave this way or that I needed his consent to do so. My decisions were my own, and I would have made them whether he wanted me to or not. (*Especially* if he didn't want me to.) But I thought I had anecdotal evidence of how my father would have behaved in the same situation. Why else had he told me, and told me and told me, about his rooftop dalliances back in the Bronx, about smoking pot and getting caught and, above all, getting away with it, if he didn't want me to know it was possible for me to get away with it, too? What else had he been trying to teach me from his example other than it is permissible and necessary to experiment with things until you find the way that you fit most comfortably into the world? How else would I know that I had measured up to him until I had a story like that of my own—a moment I could point to and say, "This is who I was before and this is who I was after"? From him, all right? I learned it by listening to him.

He had his origin story, and now I had mine.

My college career was weeks away from its conclusion, but two more years spent getting high to *Here Come the Warm Jets* by Brian Eno and *Raw Power* by Iggy and the Stooges had not been able to drown out the diligent part of my brain. As senior year dwindled to an end, its voice said to me with increasing resolve: *You must have a job before you leave this school—before you otherwise return home and are forced once again to depend on your father.* So while many of my classmates were using those delicious days after final exams and before commencement to celebrate with revelries that were more extraordinary than any they had been able to think up during the past four years, I spent my mornings traveling up to Manhattan for job interviews, clad in a patchwork of dress clothes acquired for the college application process and grandparents' funerals.

On one of these trips, I promised my father I would stop by his office and have lunch with him after my interviews. I wondered if anyone had ever worn a suit to my father's office until the day I showed up in one. As I waited to be buzzed past a rusty metal cage that lay beyond an imposing metal security door, I peered at his workplace and its towering burlap bales packed with oily animal skins. It looked more like a dungeon than ever. It had become a place that family friends would send their teenage sons to work as punishment when they got fired from their summer camp-counselor gigs for drinking on the job. While I waited for its proprietor, I sat down tenderly in a chair, trying to allow as little contact as possible between its static-charged, fur-retaining surface and my dress slacks, and still stood up with a field of unidentified fuzz clinging to my ass.

My father was up in his second-story office, his figure appearing and disappearing in its wide picture window as he spoke on the phone, pacing. He had no need for formal clothes; he was dressed in his typical uniform of a shabby white smock over a greasy flannel shirt and jeans whose expanding waistline marked the months he had kept himself free of drugs. While he was barking out a conversation with some overseas confederate—they almost always seemed to be named George—my mother traveled upstairs and downstairs from my father's private suite to a chilly underground cellar where more bales of fur were stored. When he needed for his phone conversation some bit of information that only she knew, he would cry out for her on an intercom that bellowed from every room in the building, announcing itself with a maximum-volume beep before my father's voice overtook it with a rumbling cry of "MADDY!" From anywhere in the building, you could hear his voice a split second before its electronic echo crackled through the intercom, a pair of alarms that might be sounded at any moment.

It looked like I was going to be waiting a while before my father was ready for lunch, so I parked myself in a small first-floor cubicle delineated by particleboard. As a child, I had passed the time in this same space by snapping off small pieces of the partition to see what shapes they formed. After many years and many other similarly minded occupants, the partition had been reduced to a ruin, a knee-high shambles that no longer kept the outside away from the inside. The only valuable relic still contained within its imaginary borders was a wall-length corkboard flush with old family photographs.

It was easily deduced that my father had taken most of these pictures, since he was the person least represented in them: there were a couple of snaps of him and my mother in the earliest days of their marriage, when his hair and his glasses were at their thickest and most colorful. There were a few faded black-and-white shots of my father's parents in their prime, and the original business card that my grandfather sent out when he opened his own shop, with the caption WISH ME LUCK!, and many more photos of them in their later years. My grandfather in particular struck a compelling image, lean and assured, with narrow-set eyes that refused to divulge their color and a cigar always dangling from his half-smile of a mouth.

The other pictures were almost exclusively of me and my sister: us as half-naked infants; bowl-headed toddlers racing around the old apartment or playing with toys my father loved as much as we did; gawky adolescents starting to become camera-shy; and then, except for a single picture of me at sixteen, pumping gas into my car for the first time, no more.

There was something terribly dishonest about this presentation. All these events had occurred as surely as they had been recorded. But merely displaying the photographs as if they told the complete story of a family, or even represented the most salient points of its history, was profoundly untrue. There was a guiding hand at work here, deciding what to include and what to leave out, and what was omitted were moments that no one could capture, because the person in the family who customarily took the pictures was not able or present to photograph them. No photo album can completely represent the truth, but this array was an egregious lie, constructed by and for the benefit of the family member who had the most to gain from rewriting our history.

The anger seethed and circulated inside of me the longer I waited for my father to finish his phone call, and the longer I waited, the louder he seemed to become.

"George, let me tell you something, George—George—George— shut up, will ya? Right now is when we *wait*. We. Wait. Ain't nobody ever sold nothing for more than a customer is willing to pay for it, right? Am I *right*? So that is why we *wait*. I don't care if we have to sit on this merchandise for *two. Fucking. Years*. We got it, they don't, and they're gonna come around."

What was going on up there, a spiritual revival? Where did this ersatz Southern accent come from all of a sudden? Who was this suddenly boisterous, bragging, self-assured dynamo, and what had he done with the timid, self-conscious man who could barely string together two sentences when he was on the phone with me, for all the times he bothered to call me in college? Who was he faking it for, and why couldn't he be like this with me?

[*beeeeeeeeep*] MADDY!

This was how he talked to my mother these days; this was the reward she had earned for her years of dutiful service, to be chained to him like a prisoner in the business she helped prop up during the years he could hardly run it by himself? Just because this was his business, what gave him the right to subjugate her like that, and what made him think he was entitled to have whatever he wanted at the moment he wanted it?

"George, here's the thing, George. *George!* A man don't sell when everybody else is selling and buy when everybody else is buying. Not a smart man. When everybody else is buying, you got to ask yourself: *why* is everybody else buying? Who you gonna sell to when everybody already has what you got? When *nobody* wants it, that's when you got to make your move. And then you got to wait till the market comes back. And trust me, George, trust me, it always does."

Didn't he realize how he sounded when he talked like that, how rudimentary and obvious his wisdom was? Did his buddies know how he used to spend his weekday mornings, when he was sober enough to go in to work, whining and pleading with my mother not to send him to the office? Did they know of his relentless gallows humor and how he used to joke to his own son about yearning for the sweet release from drudgery that a leap from his twenty-fifth-story apartment window would provide—how his merely uttering the word "plummet" was enough to conjure up all the terrible imagery associated with this gag?

[*beeeeeeeeep*] MADDY!

And what was I doing sitting here, letting him push me around? Hadn't I spent more than enough time waiting for him in this office? Why was he the only one whose time was valuable, who got to come and go as he pleased? I swore to the nonexistent Jewish God, if that fucking intercom went off one more time, I was walking straight out. I was leaving the office, getting right on the next train back to New Jersey, and never—

[*beeeeeeeeep*] MADDY!

I felt so right on the train ride back to school. I don't know that I'd ever felt so right about anything I'd ever done, and it felt so good to feel so right. The righteousness was tingling up my spine and twitching in the tips of my fingers. I could hardly sit still, I felt so right.

And when I got back to my dorm room and the half-dozen telephone messages left for me in the last ninety minutes, it was easy to tell which were from my father and which were from my mother.

The messages from my mother sounded like this: "David, that was not nice, what you did. We were trying to find you and we didn't know where you went. Please call your father back and apologize. You really startled him."

The messages from my father sounded like this: "David, please forgive me. Please, *please* forgive me. I didn't realize how long I had kept you waiting, and I just feel terrible. Please call me back as soon as you get a chance, as soon as you can. Please forgive me. This is your father."

I thought about not answering his calls at all, letting him wallow a little longer in the feeling he hated most, of not knowing how I felt. (It felt good to be right, but it felt even better to know that I could inflict emotions upon him that no one else could.) But while my brain still blazed with those sensations of validity and my courage was at its peak, I decided to call him back.

He still sounded a lot like his phone messages. "Please forgive me. I hope you'll please forgive me. I'm sorry, David, I'm so, *so* sorry."

"I know you are, Dad," I said, being careful not to cede any ground to him. "But I feel like this happens to us all the time. And it keeps happening to us, no matter what I try to do. If I accept your apology and say that it's okay, how do I know that things will turn out different the next time?"

"I don't know, David. What do you want me to say? What can I do to make it up to you?"

"I'm not coming back to your office. Can you come down to school to see me?"

"Sure. When?"

"What about tomorrow?"

"I'll be there."

It seemed almost unimaginable that in under twenty-four hours' notice, my father would be anywhere that wasn't his office, his couch, or his fishing boat. But true to his word, he showed up the next afternoon, looking adrift as he paced the living room of my dormitory, hands buried firmly in his pockets while he watched other people's children race to and from their lunchtime appointments and wondered where his son fit in to all of this. We tried to hug inconspicuously, and as he leaned in to kiss me on the cheek, I scanned the room for anyone who might be watching.

My father and I shared a mostly quiet lunch at a diner near school, where we ate and didn't say almost exactly what we would have eaten and not said had the meal taken place the previous day. As we walked past the large public fountain lately being used as an impromptu swimming pool by seniors who had turned in their thesis papers, he stopped and put a hand on my arm, a processional of words gathering in his throat.

He looked mostly at the ground and walked in small circles as he spoke. "David," he said, "I want you to know I've been thinking a lot lately about us. About what it must have been like for you growing up, how I wasn't there for you all the time and how confusing it all must have been for you.

"David," he said again, "I don't want you to grow up like I did. I don't want you to suffer like I suffered. I don't want you to be afraid of the things I was afraid of. I don't want you to have hang-ups. I want you to know that sex can be a wonderful experience."

It was the most perplexing thing. Every outward sign told

me that he was stone sober, and yet he was talking like he was high.

"Dad," I said, "you don't have anything to worry about. I don't want you to think that I haven't had sex—I have." I added, "I've lived. I mean, I've done things. Some things that I'd probably be embarrassed to tell you about. I don't want you to think that you did anything that kept me from having these experiences, that prevented me from enjoying them. It doesn't help to be so focused on the future. But we can still control what happens to us *right now*."

It wasn't clear he had heard me. He reached into a pants pocket and, in broad daylight, pulled out an envelope that was stuffed with a wad of twenty- and hundred-dollar bills; at a glance, I thought it must have contained at least a thousand dollars, maybe more.

"David," he resumed, "I want you to know that the business is doing well. I've made a lot of money. I want to give this to you, and I want to give you some money every month, like an allowance, that you can spend however you want. I never want you to worry about not having money when you need it."

"Dad, what does this have to do with anything?" I said, still fixated on the sum of money dangling from his hand. "I don't need this money."

"Go on," he said, "just take it."

I didn't take it, although there were many bone-dry, dead-broke days after this when I wished I had, when I would fantasize that I had asked my father to put his allowance plan in writing and have it authorized by a notary public, because that money was never tendered to me on any future date, and the allowance plan was never discussed again.

If this was the origin story of our adult relationship, its moral was dependent on who was deemed the story's protagonist. My father left that day satisfied that he had shown to himself and his son that, whether or not his assistance was needed, he would always be prepared to offer it, or so he thought. And as I watched him go home, I was more certain than ever that I did not need his help to make it in the world, or so I thought.

CHAPTER 4

I used to have this tradition, when I first moved back to New York and was living on my own, of waking up early on Sunday morning, packing a small pipe with some marijuana, and smoking it while I watched *The McLaughlin Group*. The ritual had nothing to do with the show itself—getting high hardly made the frenetic, deafening political chatter any more comprehensible or tolerable. I did it just because I could. I thought it was a show of strength, a kind of daredevil act to see how close I could come to the boundary between the weekend and the weekday and still fuck myself up, then head back in to work on Monday morning, showing no lingering effects of the lonely debauchery I'd engaged in hours earlier. But really, it was an act of weakness, a last-ditch effort to stave off that feeling of paralysis that inevitably set in around four or five o'clock on Sunday evening as it became increasingly clear that, no, the world was not going to come to an end and, yes, I would have to go back to my job the next day and work there for five consecutive days before I got two in exchange to spend as I wished (usually smoking pot). I reacted to the onset of each working week like I imagine a condemned man waits to be led to his execution: with utter cowardice and a headful of preposterous fantasies about how he might still avert the foregone conclusion of his foregone conclusion.

I don't practice this particular tradition anymore.

I had been working in Manhattan for about a year, still trying to make my way in the magazine industry, already working at my second menial assistant's job and living in my second minimalist apartment. But if I believed that I had left my family behind in suburbia completely, there were still occasional reminders that we were bound by blood and a lexicon of sardonic shorthand.

We are sometimes happily reminded of this union by the fact that my mother's and father's birthdays occur within a few days of my own, and the closest weekend to all three is the rare occasion when my parents can be persuaded to travel down to the city to celebrate with me and my sister. On one such Saturday afternoon, my sister and I arrived at a restaurant near the big, empty studio apartment I was renting on an Upper East Side block whose desolation and epic distance from the bustling center of town put the "End" in East End Avenue. At our lunch table, we found only our mother waiting to meet us. Her face was sunken and funereal, and she barely lifted her head to make eye contact. When we asked where our father was, she answered, "He's gone crazy." This was a long-standing family euphemism, by which she meant he was somewhere else in the city, and he was getting high. The three of us ate our lunch quickly and quietly, my sister and I split the check, and we kissed our mother goodbye.

Then it was Sunday, and I began the day as I usually did, sifting through my drawer of sin, second from the top on the right-hand side of the rickety IKEA wall unit that my mother had helped me put together, where I kept all my musty dime bags and resin-clogged hash pipes, finding the least filthy pipe and filling it with the least crumbly pinch of green-brown herb from the least desiccated bag, lighting it up and letting its scorching smoke race through my lungs, scraping as it went, and amble out through my nostrils. With my brain enveloped in a comfortable fog, I was about to turn on the television to watch John McLaughlin harangue Eleanor Clift and Clarence Page when my telephone rang.

With some concentration, I was able to recognize the jittery, ethereal voice on the other end as my father's. "I need your help, David," he said. "I need you to get me home."

This was a proposition I had to think about for a second. When I had been called on in the past to rescue my father, I had ignored his plea without even considering the circumstances and for no good reason other than the ironclad aphorism *You got yourself into this mess, you get yourself out*. No matter what trouble he was in now, I was in the worst possible shape to come to his aid. I was more than a little bit high myself, starting to feel anxious about a short freelance article I had pitched to *The New York Times* and was planning to report that night. Which would be harder to live with: leaving my father to fend for himself in his current condition, or explaining to a new editor that I would sometimes have to abandon assignments on a moment's notice to bail out a junkie parent?

There was something, though, about my father's repeated use of the word "need." He did not say "you must" or "you have to" or "you will." The imperative being communicated was *If you do not do this, no one else will*. (A possibly implied corollary was *I have already asked for help from other people, and they said no*.) There was something climactic and final about the whole dramatic scenario. Maybe this was what he had needed all along. Maybe if I were the one who at last redeemed him, he would never need redemption again.

"Just tell me where you are, Dad," I answered. "I'll be there as soon as I can." He gave me the street name and told me to look for a red door. Then his voice faded into silence. I went into my bathroom and splashed myself with cold water until I convinced myself that I was sober, then went outside and hailed a cab downtown.

I was wandering through the slums and schlock shops of Seventh Avenue, navigating between the long shadows cast by Madison Square Garden and irritating, penetrating shards of sunlight. I was so close to where my father had kept his office for over thirty years but could not remember ever walking this forgotten block, populated with ancient import-export wholesalers whose dusty windows still promised wholesale fabrics and novelty linings even as they were populated with nude, decapitated mannequins. Among the storefronts I found a heavy steel door swathed in a layer of chipping red paint: the gateway to a flophouse where my father had traveled from his respectable suburban home for the privilege of paying twenty bucks an hour to snort cocaine in private.

The interior of the building was not particularly unsavory but was mostly barren, a makeshift waiting area with a couple of plastic chairs, wood paneling on every surface, and a lone clerk seated behind a layer of bulletproof glass, watching a black-and-white television that was probably not tuned to *The McLaughlin Group*. Beyond this area was a narrow hallway lined with doors; streaks of light could be seen underneath each of them, flickering tentatively as their unseen occupants scuttled around. On the opposite side of every door, some aching, appalling tragedy could be playing out anonymously, and there could be a hallway like this behind every door on the block.

I asked the clerk if there was someone staying here named Gerald Itzkoff, and without asking me who I was or why I was looking for him, he directed me to my father's room.

I had never observed my father performing the complete ritual of getting high on cocaine, of consolidating his powder into fine white lines and inhaling them up his nose one by one, and on this day I still wouldn't catch him in the act. His supply was exhausted; all that remained in the room were a few rolled-up dollar bills on a nightstand, a glossy porno magazine on the floor, and a frightened old man shivering on the bed, his nostrils cemented shut with a mixture of blood and mucus, his eyelids sealed closed by some bodily fluid whose origins I couldn't even guess at. I had no idea how much coke he'd done or how long he'd been doing it, but he was coming down, and he was coming down hard. Though it was terrifying to see someone so familiar and generally functional in such a broken-down, helpless, and horrible state, I had no choice but to pretend that none of it mattered.

"Come on, Dad," I said. "Let's get you out of here."

As he stood up and walked around the room, he seemed to be vibrating in place, like a tuning fork that had been struck. He could barely see me, and I didn't want to touch him, but we worked out a system that allowed me to lead him out of the flophouse and onto the street by having him follow the sound of my voice. If I took my eyes off him or stopped calling out "Dad" every few feet, he would get distracted and try, very slowly, to shuffle away.

"David," he said, "I can't drive like this."

"Yeah, no kidding, Dad."

"You're going to have to drive me home."

He fumbled through the pockets of his putrid blue jeans, producing expired coupons and fishing licenses, scraps of paper on which he had scribbled down phone numbers and sales figures, and hundred-dollar bills folded into a kind of accidental origami, but he could not find the claim check for the garage where he had parked. We were in a neighborhood where every corner that was not occupied by a bodega, a porno video store, or a half-finished construction project had been turned into a garage, and I would have to approach every single one of them, with this lumbering, stumbling, snotty, bloody beast following me, to ask if they had his car.

At the first parking lot we passed, a group of uniformed attendants was gathered outside. "Excuse me?" I asked the least threatening-looking of them, and they all looked up at once like I'd just interrupted their craps game.

"My father can't remember if he parked his car here or not," I said matter-of-factly. "Do you recognize him? He might have come here yesterday. He's got a drug problem."

The attendant gave a short, reflexive laugh. How else was he supposed to react? You stand around on a city street long enough, you see a dozen guys shamble by in tattered clothes, their skin burned by constant exposure and their beards mangy and overgrown from inattention; they push shopping carts full of soda cans, tote their possessions in bulging, overstuffed backpacks, try to carry on conversations with their reflections in the windows they pass, listen intently to the transistor radios they carry whose batteries expired in 1978, or sit motionless on the curbside with their head buried between their legs.

You have to laugh at them, because it is dreadfully, morbidly funny to see a human being to whom you have no connection reduced to the level of a windup toy. But you don't want to know him, and you don't want to know how he ended up that way. Because if you stop believing for a moment that his slapstick misadventures have been orchestrated for any reason other than your personal amusement, you might find out this wandering old vagrant, was, hours ago, coherent and clearheaded enough to drive an expensive and dangerous American-made vehicle. You might find out he is actually someone's *father*. You might find out he is *my* father.

I did not need to visit any more garages to know that this same scene would play out at every single one. I hailed a taxi in hopes that one would be willing—in a city where a request to drive from Manhattan to Brooklyn is regarded as an ethnic slur—to deliver my father back to Rockland County. Incredibly, the very first driver I stopped agreed to do so for the proper fare mandated by the immaculate copy of the Taxi & Limousine Commission manual he kept in his glove compartment, and he even waited and watched over my father while I ran to a bank machine to withdraw money.

We were somewhere on the Henry Hudson Parkway, as I sat in the back of the cab with my father's head in my lap, when I reached into a pocket of his winter coat and pulled out an overlooked stub: the claim check for his car. His eyes were still mostly shut, and before he fell asleep, he let a final utterance dribble from his lips: "You saved my life."

From the front seat, our driver, who had deduced exactly what was going on, agreed: "You're a good kid, to do this for your father."

But how could it be that I once again found myself in this position: him, passed out in the back of a car; me, in charge of a situation I had no idea how to handle. If the shoe were on the other foot—if I were the one with the debilitating dependency and he were the one with the sober clarity—wouldn't I want him to do everything within his power to get me cleaned up? To turn his whole life upside down to make sure that mine was straightened out again? Forsake his business and the whole world he knew, if he needed to? If I was such a good kid, what was I actually doing for him? All I was doing today was sitting with him in a cab, and as soon as it reached its destination and dropped him off, I'd have my mother drive me straight home. I just wanted to get back to my empty apartment, report my story that night, get my *New York Times* byline, build my career. I wasn't willing to sacrifice anything. When you got right down to it, I was a pretty goddamned lousy kid.

When I wanted my drugs, at least I didn't go about scoring them in such an undignified manner. All I had to do was wait for a friend to throw a party, and then I'd show up and wait again until the witching hour when the timid teetotalers had gone home for the night and the drinkers had drunk their fill, when the pot pipes would be passed around and smoked in plain view of everyone who could still see straight. When a party could not be convened, I would call my delivery service: I would dial a beeper number, leave my phone number in return, and wait for someone to return the call, usually a gruff male voice that would state simply: "I'm returning a phone call." Within thirty minutes to an hour, I would be greeted at my front door by a dreadlocked young man or woman with a gym bag full of tiny translucent plastic cases packed to the brim with a sticky green crystalline algae, so potent that one bowlful would send me reeling for four or five hours, and I was warned to never, ever smoke it in a joint.

The process was chic and civilized, so routine and stripped of embarrassment—not like the desperate, demeaning groveling that my father undertook when he wanted to get high, scrounging from door to door and dealer to dealer, scrambling to find the cheapest, most isolated place where he could light himself up in private. It was a damn shame when that delivery service stopped returning my pages, for reasons I never found out. (Whom do you call for customer service?) But my supply problems were quickly rectified: I started buying from a friend's roommate, a flabby ex–frat boy who liked to walk the apartment bare-chested in backward-turned baseball caps and boxers that barely constrained his hairy belly. He was gregarious, fond of high-fiving people for any occasion, and never worked at a day job or stopped watching his big-screen TV long enough to leave his apartment. He was always available, willing to entertain at all hours, and, for a price, provide access to a metal cookie container in which he kept his entire inventory: plastic bags full of marijuana and crumpled chunks of aluminum foil that contained something else.

One afternoon, in the course of a typical transaction, I impulsively told him that in addition to my customary bag of weed, I would also like to purchase one of the foil chunks. He slapped me five as he pressed one into my palm, and I hurriedly stuffed it in my pocket. After hastening home to my empty apartment, I laid out my purchases on the dinner table and tore into the foil as if a suffocating child were trapped inside it. Its contents were slightly different than I expected: not a pile of white power but a small chunk of solid cocaine.

I looked at it for a while, unable to unlock its mysteries or extract its narcotic properties with only my eyes. Was I supposed to smoke it? Was I meant to shove the whole thing up my nose and wait for it to take effect? Should I just leave it on the mantel as a conversation piece, to prove to houseguests that I owned a small chunk of cocaine? It was supposed to be a totem of the adult experiences I was allowed to partake in, and instead, it sat there mocking me: the hardest controlled substance I had ever purchased, and I had no idea how to use it.

This was not the closest cocaine had ever come to my sinus cavities. Some had gone up my nose quite recently, in fact. Weeks ago I had been on a corporate retreat in Jamaica with my magazine colleagues, the last such time the publishing industry was so flush with cash that it could afford to pack off its employees on Caribbean vacations that were somehow supposed to lead to higher-quality media products. It was on one of those nights when our group had gathered to drink piña coladas and carouse in the living room of a stately Jamaican villa. When a small reconnaissance party split off from that group to smoke pot in a bedroom, I followed them, and when a smaller group split off from that group to sneak into the bathroom, I followed them, too.

In the available space, three or four of us were crowded around a toilet, where, on its tank, a female coworker was using her American Express Gold Card to separate a pile of cocaine into discrete, organized lines. She took the first snort, ran her forefinger under her nose, and massaged her nostrils. Another colleague did the same, and then another, and finally, there was only one line left on the tank and only me to inhale it. Without hesitation, I leaned in, trying to coordinate which nostril I would breathe through and which I would press shut with my thumb. It took more force than I realized to draw the drug into my nose, and when I lifted my head, there was still a small trail of cocaine residue that lingered like bread crumbs to mark the path. But my innocence was gone.

I waited for some profound shift in my consciousness—to receive even the tiniest glimpse or taste of whatever it was my father

found so enthralling that he had rededicated his life to its constant pursuit. Other than the mild intoxication I had brought into
the bathroom with me, and the deepening shame with which I exited, I left feeling no different than when I entered.

The defeat was still fresh in my mind when I brought my first
fragile cocaine rock home from the drug dealer in its swaddling
foil clothes. A female friend of my named Jana had recently come
back into my life. She and I had worked for the same magazine,
though not at the same time: when I showed up there, she was
leaving to live in Los Angeles; after a few months there, she
packed up again and headed to Australia. She was a funky and
free-spirited Jewish girl who knew she had this Jewish boy
wrapped around her finger, and the fact that she did not need me
in her world—that I was not a sufficiently compelling incentive to
keep her from upending her life every few months and moving
thousands of miles away—only made me want her more. On
breaks from her adventures, she would occasionally return to
New York and we'd pal around platonically, but between her fear-
less globe-trotting and my passive hope that things would naturally fall into place, no more ever came of it. I was determined to
change that on this visit.

We had spent the evening at a screening for a new George
Clooney movie, which I knew would soften her up enough that
she could be convinced to make the lengthy journey back to my
apartment.

"*How* far?" Jana asked when I explained to her the distance between Sutton Place and East End Avenue. Even in my native New
Yorker's mind, it sounded far.

"I have something there to show you," I said. "Trust me, you'll
like it."

"Okay," she said with a devilish chuckle. I liked this newfound boldness that my untested drug supply had provided me, and she did, too.

If Jana thought we were headed home to smoke pot and look at pictures of her recent trip to the Great Barrier Reef, I made it clear this wasn't my intent. From my dining table, I retrieved my wad of foil, where it still sat next to the napkin holder. "Look what I just bought," I said to Jana as I unwrapped the foil and displayed its chunky, chalky contents.

"Oh my God," she said with sly surprise, and as decorously as one would butter a dinner roll, she produced a nail file from her purse and began shaving away at the crystals, creating little piles of powder that she gathered into lines with another American Express Gold Card. With a snort, the first line disappeared up her nose, and then a second, and a third, and then finally, she let me try a couple, too.

This time it worked. The effect was unlike anything I had experienced in any previous state of consciousness: I did not feel dizzy, dazed, or distant; I was not hallucinating or mixing up my senses. I felt like I had been plugged in to myself and, in doing so, had tapped in to an aquifer of adrenaline and testosterone that was laying dormant for over a decade, accumulated through a lifetime's aversion to organized athletics, gym workouts, or any activity more strenuous than videogames. I was happy and proud to be me, infinitely confident and unafraid of anything, and brimming with more energy than I knew what to do with. But I knew exactly where I wanted to put it.

Jana was lying on my couch, looking back at me through needful, half-open eyes, and suddenly, her body started looking like an elaborate instrument panel that I had rarely gotten my hands on but which I knew exactly how to use. I started peeling off her clothes as if they were made from tissue paper, latching on to an ample breast with one hand while pawing at her pubic mound with the other, all the while in utter disbelief that *she was actually allowing me to do this to her*. As I immersed my face between her legs, her tiny moans and gasps gave way to a soft, uncertain entreaty to stop. Whether or not I wanted to heed it, she abruptly sat up and ran into my bathroom, where she began throwing up.

Within a few minutes, Jana returned to the room, unashamed. "See what happens when you get me too excited?" she said before climbing into my bed and passing out. She had taken off her remaining clothes and was dressed in one of my old college T-shirts, which barely came down to her waist. At its hemline, a few small hairs poked out from underneath, a teasing reminder of the anatomical bits that had been both my inspiration and my undoing on this night.

We woke up late the next morning, groggy and sick, and traded shy, embarrassed laughs as we passed each other going to and from the bathroom. I saw Jana with decreasing frequency over the months and years that followed, and we never spoke of this incident even once.

Here is how a house of cards begins to collapse. You build its foundation on a layer of unstable ground and add each tentative tier with a meticulous process of indifference and neglect, observing in disconnected fascination as each wobbly story is assembled atop a previous one, well beyond the point where your empirical understanding tells you that the fragile structure should be able to support itself. Then, with an inevitable tug, it starts to buckle and heave, and you watch with a mixture of defeat and amazement as it goes down and the familiar pieces you used to construct it come hurling back at you, as the whole enterprise spreads wider and sinks lower without ever finding a boundary or a bottom.

Months had passed since my meaningless rescue of my father from his self-imposed flophouse exile, the memory of the event added to our backlog of personal tragedy to be discussed and re-examined as soon as we found a mutually convenient time, which would be never. I had a new magazine job, an editor's title and my own private office, and a hip new East Village apartment, where I was relaxing one night only to have my modest tranquillity inter-rupted by another phone call at another odd hour. Proving that I had learned absolutely nothing from the previous episode, I an-swered it.

"I need to talk to you about something," my father told me, and right away I knew I was in trouble. I ran through the mental checklist that I had honed over the years, prepared for scenarios like these when he should call me out of the blue, designed to de-termine whether I was talking to someone who is sober or high: is his speech slurred or stuttering? Is his train of thought circuitous or disconnected, or does he drop out of the conversation for long periods of time? Does he only want to talk about his sex life? He passed all of these tests and yet something still seemed off, as if he were talking to me through a paper cup. Out of a kind of fatal-istic curiosity, I allowed him to continue.

"I want to talk to you about your aunt Arline," he said, referring to his older sister. "She was up here to visit your mother and me a few days ago in the mountains. I don't know what kind of life she has down there in the city. I think she should move up here. I think it would be good for her."

"Dad," I asked, "what does this have to do with me?"

"I need you to explain to her that she should do this," he said. "I want you to convince her that this is the right thing for her to do."

Had I applied some of the more rigorous and obscure criteria on my father-testing checklist—does he want to discuss an intensely personal situation involving his family? is he asking for help that he seems to think only I can provide? does he sound utterly convinced of his own unflinching standards of right and wrong?—I might have arrived at the red-flag moment that signaled to me: *Do not talk to this person unless you seek a frustrating, humiliating, ego-crushing conversation.* But the signs were so numerous and imprecise that half of them could still apply to my father when he was completely clean. Some days I felt like salvaging him from the messes he had created, and some days I wanted to leave him behind in the hourly motels of his own invention, and on this occasion I decided to rebel.

"I don't see why I should get involved in this," I said. "This is between you and your sister. I'm not going to do it."

With preternatural calm, my father replied, "Then you are a coward, and you are a failure."

It should be self-evident that hearing one's own father refer to oneself as a coward and a failure would be completely devastating to anyone, and yet I still feel I should explain why I found the remarks so unsettling: not because I feared he truly meant what he said. What frightened me most were the retaliatory acts I had often cycled through and savored in my mind, that I was free to perpetrate on him.

I had not only contemplated but fantasized about what my life would be like if I were to cut him off entirely. It was the same punishment he had threatened me with, turned on its head—I had nothing tangible that he wanted or that I could withhold from him, only unquantifiable commodities like love, contact, and compassion. My campaign would cost me nothing to perpetrate, but it would devastate him fully. I would be giving up nothing more than a sometime sounding board, a guy I could occasionally count on to hear out my plans for the future and then tell me all the ways they could possibly go wrong. He would be left to perpetually apologize to the rest of our family for my absence at gatherings and Thanksgiving dinners, to explain to his friends that he could not update them on my life because he did not know what I was doing, and to wonder, above all, how it was that he squandered the trust of this person who was once completely devoted to him—the boy of a thousand nicknames who used to believe that there was no rock so heavy that he could not lift it, no highway motorists so fast he could not outrace them, and no cocksucking traffic jam so fucking impenetrable and goddamn demonstrative of the fucking worthlessness of New York City that he could not curse it into a state of powerlessness.

There was no formal declaration of hostilities, only an abrupt cessation of concordance that took him several weeks to notice. First I had to explain my actions to his proxies. My mother called and, after an exchange of banalities, asked if there was any reason why I hadn't spoken to my father in all this time.

"Mom," I said, "didn't he tell you that the last time we talked, he called me a coward and a failure? I don't know what he was on, but I'm sure he was taking something or doing something. I don't know if I'll ever talk to him again."

Her voice turned cold with recognition. "I can understand why you might feel that way," she said, and I'm sure she could.

I next practiced the argument with my sister, who was deep in her studies at medical school. Some elements of the story had trickled down to her, but not the whole thing. "What's going on, David?" she wanted to know, as if I were withholding the details of some fatal accident from her.

"I don't know if I can be a part of this family anymore," I told her in my most self-aggrandizing tone. "I'll always be there for you if you ever need money," which was the one asset I inevitably equated with independence and self-reliance. "I'll be there for whatever you need from me. I think from now on we'll have to learn to take care of each other and look out for ourselves." Whatever I said and however I said it must have been pretty convincing, because she started to cry.

These practice confrontations were not enough preparation for facing down the man himself. He caught me off-guard with another of his sudden phone calls, this time when I was at work.

He had the opportunity to say only one thing to me, but it was enough. "David," he said, and I could just about hear the tears welling in his eyes, "are you going to stop loving me?"

In my private office, I could have closed the door behind me and said whatever I wanted without fear of being overheard. But I didn't say anything in reply. I simply hung up the phone. In the moment it felt courageous. And when I look back on the course of my life—not just the times when I could have supported my father but elected not to, out of spite or anger or confusion, but all the sins I've been responsible for, all the stains that will never be fully cleansed from my soul, all the acts of deceit and larceny, guile and ruthlessness, I've committed in my own self-interest that I dare not ever confess—I think it may have been the cruelest and most terrible thing I've ever done.

CHAPTER 5

I was talking to my mother in a stolen moment when I could be certain she wouldn't try to pass the phone to my father or allow him to listen in on the conversation when she made the suggestion. "I think you and your father should go into therapy," she said.

Setting aside the accusatory, slightly satisfied way she said this, something about her advice sounded right to me. For all the times I had tried to make my father understand that the past didn't matter—that previous disputes between us were no reason to conclude the bond between us was broken beyond repair, and previous reconciliations no reason to assume that it would always remain intact—now was my chance to show him that I meant what I said, or that I meant what I always intended to say anyway.

We didn't have to be one of those parent-child pairings who spent their adult lives wondering what *happened* to their dynamic without realizing that it was always, perpetually *happening*—whatever it was that we once had, we could always get it back, and

we could always create it anew. We didn't have to treat our relationship so delicately, as if it were some exotic electronic device
with a baffling array of buttons, any of which threatened self-
destruction if you pressed the wrong one. We had to experiment
with using this device, and any time we could not figure out how it
was supposed to operate, all we had to do was unplug it and plug it
back in again. And we could do it over and over, as many times as
we needed to, until we got it working the way it was meant to.

"Yes," I said to my mother. "Yes, I will. Yes. Can you arrange
this for us?"

As soon as I agreed to do it, I became extremely frightened
about the process I had just consented to. The harder I tried to
avoid cliché in my life, the more inevitably I ended up fulfilling it.
Now here I was, perpetuating the tradition of being so impotently
unable to solve my own problems that I had to turn to a total
stranger for help, doled out in one-hour increments. And once I
had been in therapy, I could no longer say that I'd never been in
therapy; my personal belief that I was the sanest member of my
family would be that much harder to hang on to.

By agreeing to participate in therapy with my father, I was basically admitting that I was just as messed up as he was. *This guy*, I
always knew, needed therapy. But me, too? Really? For all the
things I had ever done to excess, at least I had the good sense to do
them in private, in a way that didn't interfere with anybody else's
life. But once I was poked, prodded, and picked apart in that therapist's office, what horrible and long-denied truths about myself
would emerge after the superficial layer of infallibility was peeled
off of me? What if, for all the suffering I blamed him for inflicting
on me, I had perpetrated as much pain on him?

The psychiatrist's office was in a big midtown skyscraper of
steel and glass, and his waiting room was all right angles and oak

finishes. I arrived there well before my father, and if I thought I was nervous, he looked positively panic-stricken. He rarely came to New York anymore, having moved his fur business nearer to his summer home in Monticello a few years earlier, and in that time he appeared to have forgotten how to live among civilized society. He showed up in a T-shirt, sweatpants, and a windbreaker, probably the first things he'd grabbed when he woke up that morning, or maybe the same clothes he'd worn to bed the previous night. His hair was ghost-white and mangy, and he was unshaved, and every part of him twitched and tingled at its highest state of alertness, like he was about to be interrogated by the police for a crime he knew he'd committed. When he saw me already waiting, he spoke my name and reached out to embrace me or shake my hand, but I rebuffed him.

The psychiatrist was a thin man in a suit, with a full chestnut beard and a gentle but clinical demeanor, and he consistently mispronounced my father's name.

"Mr. Itz-off," he began, "do you want to tell me why the two of you are here today?"

"Well," my father said, turning to me, "maybe you want to—?"

I recounted the story of his confrontational phone call, the insults leveled at me, and the mystery of what substance or substances had elicited them from him. "Do you know," I said, "that he still hasn't apologized to me for this? And I still don't even know what he was on at the time."

"Is this true, Mr. Itz-off?" the doctor asked. "Did you say this to him? Were you high at the time?"

"I don't know," my father answered, which surprised me more than if he'd admitted it or denied it outright. "I suppose it's possible. I'm sure if that's how he remembers it, then it probably happened."

"Probably?" I said, incredulous. "Do you see," I said to the therapist, "how he's already trying to absolve himself of responsibility for his own actions?"

"I'm not saying it didn't happen," my father continued. "I just can't imagine what I might have been on. That's not how I talk when I'm high. If I said it, I didn't mean it."

"I'm not so sure," I said. "Usually, the things you say when you're high, you mean them as intensely as possible." I started to cry. The therapist silently extended a box of tissues in my direction.

Seated in his chair, my father clutched at the zipper of his windbreaker like it was a rosary and attempted to change the subject. "Do you know what a willful child he can be?" he said, extending at me a finger that he had been gnashing on moments earlier. "Do you know that three years ago, I moved my business up to the mountains? Three years ago, and in all that time, *he* hasn't visited my new offices."

"Dad," I said, "what does that have to do with *anything*?"

"Is that right?" the doctor asked me, trying for the moment to placate my father. "Have you never been to his new offices?"

"It's true," I said. "His offices always make me really uncomfortable."

"And why do you think that might be?" the doctor asked.

"Because," I said, "they are always run-down and ugly. They always smell terrible. And they have always been places where he goes to get high." I started to cry again.

My father gave me a dismissive wave of his hand. His breathing was heavy, and he was constantly crossing and uncrossing his legs. I had reached a conclusion that had been building up in my mind like a bomb, and I decided to detonate it.

"You know what?" I said. "I think you might be high right now."

My father leaped to his feet with such force that it rattled the diplomas and citations on the therapist's walls and shook the trophies in his display cabinets. "It's not true," my father insisted. "I am not."

"Calm down, Mr. Itz-off, calm down," the doctor said, but his repeated urgings made my father angrier still.

"I'm *not* gonna calm down," he said. "I'm *not*. I'm not gonna be accused of being high when I'm not."

"I have to say," the doctor said, "your behavior has been very erratic from the start of this meeting. I would like to recommend that you take a drug test."

"Fine," my father said, rolling up his sleeves. "Let's settle this. We'll see who's right. Give me a cup and I'll take it into the bathroom."

"Not now, Mr. Itz-off," the doctor said. "After the meeting."

"No," he demanded. "I want to take care of this now. You don't have a cup? Fine. I'll go piss in my hands." He held out his palms as if begging for charity.

Thus our first joint therapy session came to a close. After writing the doctor a check for his four-hundred-dollar fee, my father approached me outside his office doors. "I'd like to talk to you alone," he said. "I'd like to settle this, you know, between ourselves."

"No," I told him. "I don't want you riding down with me. I don't want you following me. You wait for me to leave, and then you take your own elevator."

A few days later, I learned from my sister that on his drive home from this appointment, my father got into a car accident. He walked away uninjured, but his SUV was totaled. It was agreed that we would not see this same doctor again.

After further research, my mother came back to me with a new suggestion. On the advice of my aunt, the same one whose unwillingness to relocate herself to the Catskills had inadvertently triggered the fight, she had located an institute on the Upper East Side that specialized in therapy for families dealing with substance-abuse problems. She made an appointment for me and my father there, and I found myself blithely looking forward to this visit as if the previous attempt at psychotherapy had never occurred. But I was bothered by a couple of inscrutable omens that preceded it.

First, after having recommended this new institute for me and my father, my aunt abruptly reversed course and sought desperately to talk us out of going there. Her argument hinged on the fact that the facility charged only seventy-five dollars for each session. How good a job could its staff members do, she said, if they got paid so little? Wouldn't we be better off, and get higher-quality attention, if we went somewhere more expensive?

Then, on some sleepless night, I happened to turn on the television in time to see a cable documentary about this same institute. Three couples had agreed to be videotaped during their therapy sessions and in follow-up interviews: a boyfriend and girlfriend, a husband and wife, and a mother and daughter. One by one their relationships unraveled: the boyfriend and girlfriend were both cheerful, severe alcoholics, missing work and losing jobs to go on benders for days at a time; by the end of the show, they had broken up without diminishing their addictions in the slightest. The mother was no longer on speaking terms with her daughter at the documentary's end and did not even know where she was currently living. I didn't stick around long enough to find out what happened to the husband and wife. I remained resolute in my belief that my father and I would somehow beat the odds. I just had to remember not to let anyone film our sessions.

Encouragement was coming from other places as well. A few months before, I had created a page for myself on Friendster, a website where people were invited to set up profiles for themselves, fill them with photographs and lists of their favorite books and movies, and see how many other people's profiles they could connect themselves to. Then I abandoned the project, having concluded that online social networking was a passing fad. But even when left unattended and ignored, this little Web page was doing more for my dating life than I ever could. One day, through absolutely no effort on my part, I received an email message from a young woman who said she had read something I had written and enjoyed it so much that she had sought me out and discovered we had a friend of a friend of a friend in common and, by the way, would I want to meet her for a drink some night? She probably felt as excited and frightened and ridiculous writing that note as I did reading it.

But I could see from the photograph on her page—as easily as she could see from the one on mine, in which I wore a T-shirt with the slogan TIJUANA: CITY OF TOMORROW—that this person posed no obvious threat. She had adorned her profile with her actor's head shots: two professional black-and-white pictures, one Smiling, in which she wore a big white sweater and looked like a model in an I-learned-to-live-with-herpes advertisement; one Serious, in which she wore a black tank top and showed a lot of skin. She had short blond hair and intense eyes that felt like they were looking directly at me from my computer screen, and I was very, very curious.

Our first date did not promise much; we met at a bar, and she said she was glad I wasn't as short as I'd described myself. We drank and talked, and I walked her home at the end of the night, expecting so little that I did not even react when she leaned in and kissed me good night.

We agreed to see each other a second time, and this meeting was very different. It had an energy to it, one I could sense right away when I met up with her at a Ukrainian diner in my East Village neighborhood. I told her how clearly I could see her in the light of the restaurant and how pretty she was that night, and she said, "Oh," and shyly smiled. Her name was Amy, and she was the first woman I had ever known who did not become angry or suspicious when I told her she looked good. She must have been nervous, because she ordered a plate of French toast and a glass of bourbon for dinner. We ate and drank and talked, and walked around the neighborhood and kissed. And at the end of the night, she clearly wanted me to invite her up to my apartment, but I told her no, not yet.

"I want to be the kind of person you deserve," I told her. I wasn't sure why I said it, except it sounded good—like the sort of thing you say to someone who needs further convincing to sleep with you, not to someone you're trying to talk out of the proposition.

So Amy put her arms around me and clutched me to her so tightly that I could feel her leather jacket crush and crumple itself upon my body. It was the action of someone who badly needed to be held and who knew how badly I wanted to hold her. There would be plenty of weeks and months to come for our resistances to wear down and our false fronts to erode, and for all the terrible and embarrassing truths about ourselves that we hid from each other in these earliest encounters to make themselves known.

But for now, and for everything awful and unwanted that we knew about ourselves, what we represented to each other was possibility—a window, however small, in which we might be able to make just one other person see us as the people we'd always wanted to be seen as, the people we always believed we could be.

If you could be a new person to someone who never knew you, could you be that same new person to someone who had known you for your entire life?

The first session with the new therapist was scheduled on a Saturday morning, in an inconspicuous brownstone I had passed many times on my wanderings in the East Seventies, near a subway station I frequently used and a deli where I often stopped for sandwiches, never knowing of the harrowing, heart-wrenching drama that was going on right next door while I waited for my Reubens and potato salads. Past its front door and beyond a security desk, a ground-floor living room was furnished mostly with diversions for children: tiny plastic chairs, half-filled-in coloring books, mismatched toys, and sullen stuffed animals. I was alone, so I worked on a crossword puzzle until my father arrived, and together we rode up to the townhouse's top floor in an elevator so cramped that we could not fit together in the car without my father's belly pressing up against me.

We were welcomed into a small private room smelling of fresh paint by our new therapist, a woman—by my father's demands, as he refused to see another male therapist after our previous meeting—who introduced herself as Rebecca but whom my father addressed as Becky. She was an Asian woman of roughly my height, slight and unimposing, with a short haircut. She was young, no older than thirty, and had a master's in social work and was working toward a doctorate, a degree that would presumably be awarded to her upon her successfully reconciling me and my father.

Her first words to us were tentative but well rehearsed. "What we do here is a kind of modified version of couples' therapy," she said in a soft but formal voice that betrayed the slightest of accents. "Now, maybe you do not think of yourself as a couple, but in a way, you are. It's true, a lot of the people we see here, they are married or dating. Husbands and wives, boyfriends and girlfriends. They chose to be together, and they can choose to break apart if they want.

"You are family. You did not choose to be together. You cannot choose to break apart. But you did choose to be here today. That tells me that you value each other, that you value your relationship. That you want to work on it together to make it better.

"A lot of relationship problems," she continued, "are communication problems. So that is what we're going to focus on in here, communication. We're going to work on active listening, which unfortunately sounds like what a lot of people think of when they think about therapy. You say to someone, 'I hear you when you say . . . *this*.' Or 'When you say that, it makes me feel . . . *this*.' It can be weird to get used to. But sometimes when things haven't been working for a long time, we convince ourselves that they are working anyway. And then we don't know where they first went wrong. So we must start from the beginning, from the simplest, most basic steps, and build up from there. You are a father, and you are a grown son, and maybe you do not want to think about starting something new, starting all over again. But you have to start from the same beginnings in order to end up in the same place."

There were two additional conditions that Rebecca revealed to us about her therapy sessions. First, she said she wanted us to write up a contract that would spell out all the goals we wanted to achieve during our time with her, so we could track our progress and determine when our therapy was complete. I liked her optimism—she seemed to believe the process could actually conclude well, without one of us quitting or dying. But this condition made my father exceedingly nervous, even after she told him he would not have to supply his suggested language for the contract until next week.

"I think I'm gonna need my wife's help with this one," he told her with a nervous chuckle. "I haven't written a complete sentence since grade school. They would ask me to write what I did on my summer vacation—I would turn the paper in blank."

Second, Rebecca explained that all of our sessions would be videotaped, so that each week she could share these tapes with a panel of trained psychologists who were instructing her—a kind of therapy for the therapist, to remind us what tender and inexperienced hands we had trusted to tend to our mutual mental health. It was a direct violation of the one rule I had established for myself a few days earlier: do *not* let someone videotape your therapy sessions. And yet I allowed it to pass without the least bit of protest, because a person of authority had suggested it, and because I was too busy silently studying the other details of the room: the plastic dinosaur toys on the bookshelf, the halogen lamp that leaned a few degrees away from perfect verticality.

At Rebecca's request, I once again performed my recitation of the recent events that had landed us here: the original phone call from my father (injurious), his frame of mind and the substances he may have been on (mysterious), the aftermath (apocalyptic). By now I had my presentation of the story down cold, knowing exactly what to emphasize in order to elicit maximum sympathy from my audience.

"Why do you think this bothered you so much?" Rebecca asked me as the camera continued to roll.

"I've just never heard him talk like this to me before," I said. "Either he didn't mean any of it, which would be pretty bad, or he did, which would be worse. I don't know what to root for here."

I expected her to say that I was right and he was wrong and be done with it, but she wouldn't give me such easy satisfaction. "David," she asked, "what does your father usually talk about when he gets high?"

Now, that was an interesting question, one that I couldn't recall anyone asking me before. But I didn't have to think long about my answer.

"Usually, he wants to talk about his sexual anxieties," I said. "How much fear he had about sex when he was growing up and how he never wanted me to go through the same thing. How he didn't want me to be afraid of sex and how, when I was younger, he even offered to hire a prostitute for me if I wanted."

Hearing this, my father began to choke up. Having been made to listen to my remembrances of the terror, unease, and confusion that he had instilled in me at a tender age, he now was crying tears of joy. After all these years he had been struggling to make himself understood, using drugs to give himself the courage to do so, it turned out that not everyone was dismissing his tirades as the rantings of a lunatic. There had been someone listening all along, trying to connect the dots as best he could, from the time he was a little boy to the day he sat down, as a man, with his father in a series of therapists' offices.

"It's true, it's true," my father said, weeping.

Not knowing our backstory beyond what I had already told her,

Rebecca was confused by my father's reaction. "Why does this make you cry, Mr. Iss-i-koff?" she asked. I assumed that over time she would learn to pronounce our name correctly.

"Well," he said, "it probably has something to do with David." He handled the last word gently, as if placing it on a pillow. From the delicate, reverential way he intoned the name, I knew he wasn't talking about me.

My father rarely talked about his brother, David, anymore. If the name came up in conversation, it was usually by accident; it was a side street he traveled only on unintended meanderings, one where he immediately reversed course and sped away whenever he found himself on it. The few family photographs in which I had seen David, looking young and vital with a dirty-blond pompadour and the slightest of overbites, like a Jewish John F. Kennedy, had been hung in my grandparents' apartment but never in my parents' home. The only relics of his that I had, passed on to me after my grandmother's death, were a couple of Edward Hopper—esque paintings of deserted storefronts and seascapes, signed with the diminutive "Davi." Whatever else my father possessed or knew about David, he rarely ever shared it for fear that what was left was so fragile it would dissolve in the sunlight.

"He was only eighteen when he was in the accident," my father said to Rebecca. "He'd never really lived away from me or away from our parents. I don't know what he'd experienced. I don't think he ever even had a girlfriend."

None of this meant, however, that my father had stopped thinking about David or stopped loving him. Indeed, he loved him so much that he named his first son after him, and he fought for that name, even after his sister had given it to her son, and after that son was discovered to be autistic, and after the rest of his family had concluded that it was a cursed name and should be left alone. He loved David so much that he perhaps believed at times that his son really was his lost brother brought back to life, with all the same needs, desires, and anxieties that my father had been unable to help him fulfill, from when they shared a bedroom every night until the day my father went off to college.

"Dad," I asked him, "are you afraid because you think David died a virgin?"

"Yes," he answered with sudden and unexpected relief. "Yes."

Rebecca must have been pretty satisfied with her work, because the two men who, an hour ago, had entered her room, with its toy dinosaurs, its video camera, and its slanted halogen lamp, on the verge of outright hostility were embracing for the first time in many months. Our new clarity had cost us all of seventy-five dollars, which my father paid for with a business check he had safely stowed in the front pocket of his flannel shirt like a good-luck charm. And did I mention this was only our first session?

My father was in such a positive mood afterward that he drove me home, and his exuberance was making him antsy. At every turn and traffic light, he asked me for directions through the city where he had lived for fifty years, from the recently expired parking meter on the Upper East Side where he had left his car to the Ukrainian diner in the East Village where we stopped to eat lunch, the same setting where Amy had ordered her bourbon-and-French-toast dinner on our victorious second date. No one had instructed my father and me to spend any additional time together outside our therapy sessions, but it seemed like a natural way to keep alive our forward momentum, a onetime act that could easily become a regular tradition if we applied a minimal amount of effort. I ordered the first of what would be, over the next several weeks, many roast-beef club sandwiches on white toast with Russian dressing on the side, while my father ordered scrambled eggs, soft, and a cup of coffee with half-and-half and Sweet 'N Low, then a second cup the same way, to be brought out when the meal arrived. He spoke so rapidly that not even a waiter with a perfect grasp of English and a pencil and pad in his hand—a luxury we did not enjoy that morning—could have kept pace with him. He made his demands with such specificity that I feared our fragile harmony would be ruined if the order wasn't fulfilled to his exact liking.

While we waited for our food, my father's excitement metamorphosed into familiar agitation. "David," he said as he stripped a paper wrapper from a plastic straw and tore it into tiny pieces, "we've got to think of a way to communicate with each other when we're in that room—a way we can signal to each other when we've gone too far or when one of us has said something that offends the other person. Because if this is going to work, don't I have to feel free to say whatever I want in there? But whatever we say in there, it's got to stay in there and not interfere with our relationship out here."

"Don't worry about it, Dad," I said. "I'm sure we'll figure out something. Now that we've gotten things back on track, I don't see why either of us would do anything to screw it up again. I can't imagine what you could say in there that would set me off again." At the time, I really couldn't.

CHAPTER 6

What did he say? How did it go?

What was that horrible, gut-clenching couplet he used to recite in the middle of every argument, as if to show that no bit of wisdom could be contradicted if it had meter and cadence—as if to prove that nothing that rhymed could ever be wrong?

Was it this?

A man against himself convinced
Is of the same opinion since.

No, that surely doesn't sound like anything my father would say. But if that's the wrong verse, why can't I remember the right one? If I can retain everything from the complete lyrics of the Beatles to the opening stanzas of *The Canterbury Tales*, from the strange, synaptic wallpaper patterns in the hallway of my childhood apartment building to my complete history of telephone numbers, why can't I keep track of two simple, stinking lines of superstitious poetry?

I convinced myself that I'd always remember them, which is another way of saying I assumed I'd never be rid of them. But when I thought I was holding on to the words themselves, I was only savoring the intensity of my annoyance with them, congratulating myself for how much shrewder I was than the man who spoke them. Maybe I've lost them for good, and I'm surprised at how sad that makes me feel.

I was no more diligent about keeping track of the year that my father and I spent together in therapy. At the start of the process, I thought I might keep a diary that would chronicle our amazing journey—our rehabilitation from a pair of relatives who no longer shared anything more than some blood and chromosomes and an affinity for the Yankees and *Mad* magazine, to a loving and fully functional parent and child. But I got lazy.

I was so sure that the intensity of the sessions would burn themselves into my brain, but even a glance at the sun eventually fades from behind your eyelids. All that remains of the experience is partial and episodic: I know that these events occurred, but the order in which I string them may reflect the sequence in which they happened or the sequence in which it is most convenient for me to organize them. The memories dangle like charms on a bracelet that I stashed in some old tchotchke drawer, all knotted and tangled. But they're all I have left.

I. The Movie

In his old age, before he died, Robert S. McNamara wore his righteousness in every part of him that was visible on the movie screen. He was wrinkled and desiccated, still mowing what few strands of hair remained on his head into the same orderly, angular cut he had favored since at least 1961. The pitched, exuberant voice he once emitted, when he stood beside John and Robert Kennedy on the winter morning his selection to the president's cabinet was announced, had been worn down by time's millstone to a bitter growl.

My father and I had been told by our therapist that we should start reengaging in more traditional social activities outside her office. A movie seemed a safe starting point; all he and I would have to do was sit and watch the screen. But it was also a potentially ambitious and even dangerous first date for us. It has long been my father's custom, after having been seated in a darkened room for any period of time, to fall into a deep and relaxing sleep. The challenge fell to me to select a film with enough action to keep him awake, yet with the least amount of on-screen sex or nudity to cause any embarrassment on my part. So I chose a Sunday matinee of *The Fog of War,* an Errol Morris documentary about McNamara and his role as the architect of the Vietnam War.

McNamara seemed just the right subject, guaranteed to bring our blood to equal boil, yet for opposite reasons. I had learned to despise him for the suffering he had inflicted; my father spoke his name like a swearword because he felt he didn't inflict enough—that he did not use every means at his disposal to prevail in a battle that my father never stopped believing was winnable. I felt that McNamara had contributed to a world where war was dehumanized and destigmatized, perpetual and inevitable, while my father genuinely regretted never serving in the war that McNamara helped create.

Had I made the effort to look for it, I could have found palpable and vivid evidence of my father's politics in our therapy sessions, even when not a word of politics was discussed. It was all in the boisterous and certain way he conducted himself, the way his voice filled up the tiny room, and the expressive flailing of his arms and slapping of his hands against his lap that accompanied his most passionate rants: he might open a morning's discussion with a tribute to the new computer he had just purchased and the attentive technical support he was receiving from the company, or segue into a side-by-side comparison of my and my sister's financial acumen ("This one saves fifty cents out of every dollar that comes in; the other one spends every penny she's ever earned"), and finish up maybe with a beloved anecdote about something a friend had once said to him when they were drunk at a party: "He said, 'I'd rather that my son have sex with my wife than have sex with her myself.' I thought that was beautiful." That was supposed to illustrate, I think, the extent to which fathers will sacrifice for their sons ("Someday, when you have a son of your own, you'll see").

There was no need for me to go in search of hidden clues to my father's emerging political bent when the evidence had been accumulating for years. Between the confluence of the 9/11 attacks and his self-imposed exile with my mother in the Catskills, the ascent of the Internet, and the emergence of twenty-four-hour conservative news channels, he had created a hermetically sealed environment in which the only depictions of the outside world he engaged with were those expressed in all-capital letters and at maximum volume. His devotion to cable-TV news had become its own kind of addiction; its programs blared simultaneously from multiple screens within his house, putting him to bed at night, staying on while he slept, and waiting for him when he woke up in the morning. The man who was epically fearful of expressing himself in writing, and who trembled at the thought of having to write anything more on a page than his own name, now had a limitless supply of prefabricated chain-email messages appearing in and being forwarded from his account that, with the click of a button, could be passed along to his business contacts, his friends, and his son, to alert them that

estrogen from birth control and morning-after pills is causing male fish across America to develop female sex organs—and environmentalists, who are overwhelmingly "pro-choice," have helped cover it up

and

America has been the best country on earth for black folks. It was here that 600,000 black people, brought from Africa in slave ships, grew into a community of 40 million, were introduced to Christian salvation, and reached the greatest levels of freedom and prosperity blacks have ever known

and

the fanatics rule Islam at this moment in history while the "silent majority" is cowed and extraneous.

Lately, in our therapy sessions, he had been talking a lot about the tremendous guilt he felt for never serving in the Vietnam War. His fate had been sealed on the day when he was busted for smoking pot and when his split-second response to a draft board disqualified him forever. Absent all those events, his age probably would have put him on the safe end of the eligibility curve by the time his number was called, though I remain convinced that circumstances and his lack of athleticism would have conspired to make him a name on a wall and not my father. But he was still wishing almost thirty years later that he could have participated in what was once America's most futile military folly.

I knew a single afternoon spent watching a combative, life-justifying interrogation of McNamara would not suddenly reverse the polarity of my father's political philosophy. But I thought it might teach me a few things, like: how did someone who was once so very like me come to believe the complete opposite of what I felt? How can you identify with and love a person who, in crucial situations, will behave very differently from you? How can you rely on him and trust him if he thinks these things?

I thought about this as we listened to McNamara recount his biography, his professional background steeped in corporate management and statistical analysis but devoid of any military oversight experience, and his philosophy, held then if not now, that a war could be won on paper if *we* just lost fewer men on our bombing runs than *they* did. I probed my soul for sympathy in the moments when my father would clench his fists or grit his teeth, shake his head in disagreement with McNamara, sigh an exasperated sigh, or mutter "stupid bastard" under his breath. To my surprise, he never burst into the same verbal furor elicited by the television pundits with whom he agreed or disagreed so ardently that he sometimes seemed to think he was debating them in his own living room. He said nothing back to the screen, or to me as the credits rolled while we walked up the aisle and out of the theater.

Just as we did after each therapy session, we followed the movie by retreating to our Ukrainian diner, where, unmoved by the experience, my father ordered his eggs exactly as he always did. I waited for him to bring up the movie, and when he did not, I finally asked, "So what did you think?"

"So many things, David," he said. "So many things." He wasn't yet ready to share what those things were, and I hadn't yet found a way to ask him. One prophecy from his email had come to pass: I felt cowed and extraneous, and I fell silent.

II. The Plate

Saying goodbye to my parents' house in New City, the one I had lived in after we left Manhattan, was easy. It made me glad that there are words like "final" and "never," abrupt enough to convey a sense of permanent nonexistence, even if our brains can't fully comprehend the idea. I had never thought of the house as a place of residence, just a layover between the completion of high school and the start of college, between the completion of college and the start of my real life. It was the place where I kept my old comic books and a set of weights I used only once after my father bought them for me. All I had to do was pack up the comic books and discard the weights, and when I left the house, I would be leaving it for the last time. But I leave places for the last time all the time.

For my parents, the circumstances of their forced diaspora to the Catskills were much different and the stakes much higher. An old creditor of my father's, long forgotten, had suddenly returned from financial near-death, demanding repayment on an ancient loan and the exorbitant interest payments my father had agreed to at a time when his business was not so prosperous and the notion of his living a long and healthy life seemed as laughable as the idea of his ever owning a house in the suburbs or achieving sobriety. In time a court would rule these interest payments usurious and declare the debts void, but for now my father could not take any chances: he could not claim poverty while owning two houses and three cars, and he might need a lot of money very soon.

So he and my mother sold the home where they rarely resided, knew none of the neighbors, and had no friends. They spent their last days there dejectedly packing up its contents and preparing to move them to their much smaller house in Monticello, or into cold storage alongside my father's fur. It probably occurred to them, as it did to me, that in the next instance when their earthly belongings were subjected to such a thorough inventory and relocation, they would not be available to help out.

On my final visit to that house, I went out to lunch with my father on an afternoon break from the upending of his life. As we drove around town in the car, once mine and now his, that he had unhesitatingly bought for me the summer when my previous ride, a five-hundred-dollar wreck that lacked even a cassette player, died abruptly, I was taking a victory lap in my mind: past the movie theaters I had visited on Friday nights no matter what was showing, the pizza parlors that went out of business only to be replaced by other pizza parlors, the country roads where my father had taught me to drive, and the highway where he had once nearly driven us into oncoming traffic. After we ate, we were sitting in the car when my father put his hand on my arm. "David," he said to me, "can you hold on a second?

"I'm not sure how to tell you this," he went on. "I'm not even sure I have the right to do this to you. But it's always been my policy to tell you the truth, and I feel you should know it."

"Dad," I said, "what is it? Would you just say it already?"

"Okay," he said, "here goes. A few weeks ago I went in to the doctor for a routine blood test, and when the results came back— well, they think they might have noticed something with my prostate. I have to go in for a few more tests. They said it's most likely nothing, but then again, it might be something."

"So that's it?" I said. "You got me all worked up over something that's probably nothing?"

"David," he said, much more tenderly than I had responded to him, "this is something I've been wrestling with for days. I didn't know how to tell you. I know you don't like it when you feel like you've been left out of these things, and I wanted you to know as soon as I could, as soon as I was ready to tell you."

"Yeah," I said, "but did you have to tell me like this? So much . . . drama? Maybe you need to think about how you say things like this."

"Maybe," he said. "Maybe you need to think about how you *react*."

I had planned to bring up this exchange at our next therapy session, but my father arrived with plans of his own. He began the meeting with a not unfamiliar complaint about my sister, with whom he was having difficulty communicating in the most basic sense.

"*This* one," he said, "never answers her phone. And if I leave a message, do I get a call back? Maybe two days later, maybe three. Maybe never. Sometimes it's like, I wonder, hey, do I even exist?"

"Do you think she's avoiding you?" said our therapist, whom my father still insisted on calling Becky.

"Hey, I don't know," he said. "Becky, let me ask you something. You've got a father, right? He calls you sometimes? You ever not return his phone calls?"

"Mr. Iss-i-koff," said Rebecca, "this isn't about me. Let's stick to you. Why do you think your daughter doesn't call you?"

"I don't know," he said. "But let me tell you something about my own father. Do you know that he had a glass eye? And he was always embarrassed by it. I was rifling through the glove compartment of his car one day when I found an eye that he kept in there. And later on, I told him that I had found it." He began to get choked up. "And I put my arms around him and said, 'Dad, I want you to know that I don't think any less of you because of this.' And do you know what he told me? He said, 'Gerald, if it wasn't for that damned eye, I could've been president.' And I said, 'Dad, *don't you understand that you always could?*'"

It was unclear to me how the story related directly to the issue of him and my sister, but before I could express this, he had moved on to another anecdote.

"Do you know," my father continued, "that it was my father who saved me from drugs? It was his idea to split up the business and to leave me in charge in New York while he went back to New Orleans. At the time I begged him not to do it. But he knew—*he knew!*—that it would be the best thing for me. He said, 'Gerald, I know you, and I know you're going to do whatever it takes to keep your business afloat. You're not going to let yourself go down like that.'"

Set aside, for the moment, the fact that over a decade would elapse between when my grandfather put my father in charge of the fur business and when he achieved some semblance of sobriety. Everything, it seemed, that now or ever preyed on his psyche was simultaneously issuing forth from him in a cacophonous blurt. The remembrances and the grievances were all somehow interconnected in his mind, a string he could keep pulling on and pulling on like handkerchiefs produced from a magician's sleeve. The trick in this case was getting the performer to stop.

"Dad," I interrupted, "I know all this stuff is important to you, but we're supposed to be here to talk about us."

"In all fairness, Mr. Iss-i-koff," Rebecca added, "you have been talking for a long time now. Maybe you should let David say something."

My father recoiled as if she and I had both pulled knives on him. "Hey," he cried, "isn't this supposed to be a place where I can talk about anything I want? Don't I have enough going on in my life that now I gotta fight with you two? I've got a daughter who doesn't even acknowledge that I'm a person, I'm dealing with this prostate thing, I'm losing my house." He paused, and then with all of his might: "My *plate*," he bellowed, "is *full*."

He brought his hand down as if to punctuate his declaration with a loud slam, but there was no table in front of him, so he ended up slapping himself on his leg. I closed my eyes and let a few tears slip out and caress my cheeks.

"David," my father asked hoarsely, "why are you crying?"

"I can't stand to see you get like this," I said. "It just reminds me too much of when you used to get high."

"Do you think that I'm high now?"

"No."

"Have I ever once gotten high in the last five years?"

"I don't know. I don't think so."

"Someday," he said, "you're going to have to learn that you can't hold everything against me just because I used to do drugs."

III. The Fan

The box for the ceiling fan and lamp assembly contained eleven pieces: two teapot-shaped parts that joined together to form the motor, four plastic blades with a fake wood finish, a remote control, and four ceramic fixtures to hold the lightbulbs (not included). Its retail cost at a Home Depot in Kiamesha, New York, was about ninety dollars, but its actual cost to me, as a gift from my father, was zero. He told me these things were a snap to build, and that he had previously set up several of them in his Monticello home, and I believed him. We never imagined that in the course of putting one together, we would dismantle each other.

The whole enterprise of installing the ceiling fan in my apartment had been my father's idea. He had decided on a previous visit to my boxy fifth-floor walk-up that the cool breeze generated by my air conditioner did not carry well enough from my bedroom to my living room, in the same way that he decided my upstairs neighbors, a pair of bone-thin NYU undergraduates who barely filled out their flip-flops, made too much noise as they trampled across their floor ("Are you living underneath Frankenstein?" he wanted to know). It had been a long time since my father and I had collaborated on a project requiring physical exertion: the last time had been in the 1980s, when he helped me install a hard drive in my computer, after he came home to find me attacking the device with a hammer. Since then, I told myself, I had matured.

The ritual began in my living room on a Saturday afternoon one summer after our therapy session and our customary lunch at the Ukrainian diner. We attached the fan's four blades to the motor unit and removed my old light fixture with graceful, professional ease. We brimmed with deceptive bravado, believing the task would be completed well before the afternoon's Yankees game. We would be done soon enough to watch Derek Jeter put our own crude displays of dexterity to shame while an energy-efficient fan circulated the air and cooled our exposed knees.

Our first challenge was mounting the assembled fan to the newly created hole in my ceiling, which yawned above us somewhat higher than we'd anticipated. From the basement of my brownstone, I retrieved a ladder, but my father and I could not stand on the ladder simultaneously, and one of us needed to hold the mount steady while the other person screwed it into place.

"Do you have another ladder?" my father asked.

"*Another* ladder? I'm lucky I had *one*." I went back downstairs and walked across the street to a Spanish bodega, where I borrowed a second ladder from a Bangladeshi clerk who did not even ask what I needed it for. I bought a lot of soda and Ring Dings from that place.

I had carried two ladders a total of eleven flights of stairs, and my father and I were now standing atop them at the same height, only to discover that we had a problem with the division of labor. While I held the mount, my father attempted to screw it into place with an electric screwdriver. But he could not balance the screws on the tip of the tool and drive them up into the ceiling. Each time he tried, the screws would fall to the ground, roll around on the floor, and get lost underneath furniture, to which my father would say, "Whoopst." Not "Whoops," as everyone has ever said since expressions of embarrassment and dismay were first invented, but "Whoopst," with a T at the end. "Whoopst! Whoopst!" he would say, and laugh at his own mistake.

The fan was becoming too heavy for me to hold over my head. So I jury-rigged a temporary solution by placing a pillow on my head, putting the fan on top of the pillow, and holding the fan in place with the pillow on my head, while my father continued his hopeless chore of locking in the screws.

"Whoopst! Whoopst!" he said.

When I could not bear to hear him say "Whoopst!" one more time, we switched places. The head-pillow-fan arrangement seemed too undignified for my father, so he tried to hold it up with his hands while I operated the screwdriver. I also found it difficult to screw upward, but I was able to lock one screw in place and needed to secure only three more to finish our task. That was when, to my horror, I saw that my father's arms were trembling.

"David," he said, "I gotta let go."

"Not now, Dad!" I demanded. "We're almost finished. You have to hold on just a little bit longer."

"David," he said, "I'm sixty-five years old. I'm not a young man anymore. I know when I'm beat. I gotta come down. I'm coming down." I was sweating profusely and my father even more so. We really could have used a fan to cool us off.

He let go of the heavy, half-installed contraption, leaving it to hang awkwardly from the quarter-attached mount. He descended his ladder, sat down on the couch, and began wringing out his tired arms.

I reluctantly removed the one locked-in screw and detached the fan from its electrical wiring. I set it down on the floor and looked up at the large hole in my ceiling, with lengths of wire sticking out of it, and neither a lamp nor a fan to fill it.

"Goddammit, Dad," I said. "This whole fan was your idea. I never wanted to do it in the first place. Now I have nothing. I don't have a fan. I don't even have a lamp to light this room. What am I going to do now?"

My father laughed. "David," he said, "it's not a big deal. You can hire somebody to do it for you. You can do it tomorrow."

"I think you'd better leave," I said. We didn't watch any baseball together that day. I was too defeated to return either of the ladders I had borrowed, so they stood all day in my living room beneath the ceiling hole like some art installation.

On Sunday I went on Craigslist and found a handyman who, for fifty dollars, installed the ceiling fan. He screwed the mount in place while I balanced the fan on my head with a pillow. I quickly discovered that even at its medium setting, the fan spun so quickly that it blew loose papers around my living room, and over time it was too much of a hassle to keep its fake-wood-finished blades free of dust.

A few months later, I joined a gym where a weight machine called the overhead press became my nemesis. After over a year of training on it, I was never able to lift over twenty-five pounds above my shoulders, and with each of the 3,744 reps that I estimate I did in that time, I thought of the goddamned fan with every strenuous goddamned lift. A few months after that, I moved out of the boxy apartment, making no effort whatsoever to disconnect the fan and take it with me. I hope that whoever lives there now does a more diligent job of dusting its blades than I did.

IV. The Card

There are only two practical driving routes from Monticello to Manhattan, with the only major difference between them being the choice of the Tappan Zee Bridge or the George Washington Bridge. At most hours of the day, on most days of the week, either option should deliver a traveler to his destination in a consistently reproduceable amount of time; a Monticello resident with a regularly scheduled Saturday-morning appointment in Manhattan should, with minimal practice, have no trouble arriving for this engagement as punctually as Mussolini's celebrated trains. Still, the trip presented my father with the occasional challenge.

One morning I was sitting in the lobby of our therapist's office, working systematically through a bagel and a crossword puzzle. I allowed myself one bite of the bagel for every five crossword clues solved as I waited for my father, and I tried to guess the identities of the other families I occasionally saw enter and exit. Which parent had the substance-abuse problem? The mother? The father? Both of them? What was the substance—or were there substances plural? How much did their child or children understand about what they were going through? Were they closer to reconciling than my father and I seemed to be? It was satisfying to imagine that they were much, much further away.

It was ten minutes before the start of our session, then it was starting time, and then it was ten minutes after, and then twenty. Finally, my father ambled through the institute's front door with a look on his face that seemed to ask: *Have I seen this place before?* After giving me a perfunctory, jittery hug, he walked up to the young black man who manned the security desk and laid out an array of quarters.

"Let me ask you a favor," my father said to him. "I'm parked outside at a meter that's going to expire in another couple of minutes, while I'm upstairs with the therapist. At about half past, could you go outside and put some money in it for me? It's the red Taurus just outside."

It was as if my father had walked into a bank and asked a teller to do his laundry. I did not like that he was asking the man to do a job that fell well outside his clearly designated responsibilities; the fact that he was an old white man asking a young black man didn't make it any more comfortable. All I had to do to register my discontent was let out an exasperated sigh.

My father heard it. "What?" he snapped at me.

"This isn't his job," I said. "It's not his responsibility to put quarters in your meter."

"Hey," my father said, "let him answer for himself."

The receptionist gave no response, yes or no. He just stared blankly at the quarters my father had presented to him.

"I'm saying he shouldn't have to do this, and you shouldn't put him in this position," I said, and so saying, I swept the quarters off the countertop and into my pocket.

My father and I rode together in the cramped elevator, pressed up against each other and saying nothing. He barged headfirst into Rebecca's office, and before she could chastise us for being late, my father extended his hand, instructing her to wait.

"I have something I'd like to talk about," he said. "We were just downstairs, and I was running late, and I didn't have time to put enough money in the meter. I asked the guy behind the desk if he would feed the meter for me, and my son"—enunciated as if he were saying "my tumor"—"gets mad at me. I say what business is it of his if this guy is willing to put the quarters in for me? But what do you say, Becky? Who was right, and who was wrong?"

Rebecca started to answer in a sterner voice than she typically demonstrated. "You shouldn't ask the guard to do that for you, Mr. Iss-i-koff. That's not what he's here to do."

I should have let her finish, but I interrupted: "What does this have to do with anything? Do you understand that we're not here to have Rebecca settle every argument we ever get into? Of all the things we could be talking about in the . . . thirty minutes we've got left, how does this relate to you and me?"

"Hey," my father said, "it's my money, my time, and I'm going to talk about whatever I want to talk about."

"Fine, but you're going to do it without me," I said. I exited the room and, in what felt like one continuous motion, descended the institute's long staircase, blew past the same receptionist I had been defending minutes ago, and walked out the front door.

One subway ride elapsed, and I was walking the blocks back to my apartment when my overriding sense of certainty and righteousness began to wear off. My cellphone rang, and I could see that the call was from Amy. We had been seeing each other more frequently, long enough for me to have told her that I had been going to therapy with my father and long enough for her to have known that this was the regular time of the week when I normally would be in a session. My outsize frustration that she would call me at a time when she knew I would not be reachable was outweighed by my desire for human contact, and I mistakenly took the call.

"Hi," she said cheerfully, not yet realizing that she was talking to a crazy person.

"Why are you calling now?"

"I—I was just going to leave a message," she said, startled. "Aren't you supposed to be in therapy right now?"

"I am," I said. "I was. I left."

"Is something wrong?" she asked. "Do you want to talk about it?"

"Let's just say it got really bad in there today and leave it at that."

"You sound so sad right now," she said. "Can't you at least tell me what happened?"

"I will," I answered, "at some point. But not right now. I don't think you're ready to hear it. I don't want to freak you out."

"But you wouldn't," she pleaded. "Don't you understand? I'm not going to run away from you because you've got problems."

"Not. Right. Now," I said, ending the call.

That did not go well at all. So I picked up my cellphone again and dialed my mother, hoping that she of all people would absolve me of my frustration and give me permission to end this misguided experiment.

"Mom," I said, "I can't do this anymore. He's not listening to the therapist. He's not listening to me. He won't listen to anyone."

"What can I tell you?" she said evenly. "He's a difficult, difficult man."

She called me back later that day to tell me she had been shopping in Wal-Mart and found a greeting card that she thought summed up the situation perfectly and that I would be receiving it soon.

A few days after, a simple cream-colored envelope arrived in my mailbox. Inside was a card with an illustration of Winnie the Pooh, in his au naturel A. A. Milne era, before Walt Disney compelled him to wear human clothes, holding hands with Piglet in a windy storm. A caption read, *Be brave, dear friend. You're stronger than you think . . .*

On the inside, it continued (*And you can hold my hand anytime you want*).

My mother had added a message of her own in her whispering, minuscule script, dated the same Saturday as the day I had fought with my father. It looked like she had spent many minutes carefully considering her words, and it was as much as I had seen her write in years:

Dear David—
    Did I tell you this was the perfect card.
Life is not perfect—Do not expect perfection
Even from those you love, As much as it hurts
you, & as much as it frustrates you.
Do not isolate yourself—you do not have to
be alone because of disappointment &
you can do anything "together."
    Because we care, we Love you always,

Mom

Hers was the only signature that appeared on the card, but it was enough to ensure the therapy sessions would continue for at least a few more weeks.

V. The Hall

Here is roughly how every conversation my father and I have ever had about baseball has ever unfolded:

> HIM: So are you at work right now?
> ME: Dad, I'm at home. You called me here.
> HIM: . . .
> ME: . . .
> HIM: So did you see that the Yanks traded for Johnny Damon?

Here is what I remember about the time, several years ago, when I took my father to see Game 2 of the 2000 World Series between the Yankees and the Mets. I remember purchasing the tickets on eBay, offering the seller an additional two hundred to shut down the auction immediately even though I had placed the highest bid. I remember the feeling of anxiety that amassed like lead pellets in my stomach when I saw that the tickets had no holograms, watermarks, or other fancy anti-counterfeiting features, and I believed right up until the moment when they were accepted at the gate of Yankee Stadium that I had purchased fakes. I remember how terribly cold it was that night and how distant from the action our seats were, and how, when Mike Piazza had a piece of his broken bat lobbed at him by Roger Clemens, it looked like Clemens was gently tossing it in Piazza's direction. I remember how the Mets outfielder Benny Agbayani's boast that his team would take the series in five games was rendered null and void when the Yankees picked up their second win that night, and how amazed I was at the ease with which we caught our subway ride home despite the size of the crowd that had turned out.

I just don't remember anything my father or I said to each other, if we said anything to each other at all.

A few years later, on the advice of our therapist, we came to the Baseball Hall of Fame. A bunch of nothing in the middle of nowhere is how I'd describe it. We arrived on a cool summer afternoon, expecting to find it overrun with other pilgrims, drawn by some magnetic pull transmitted through testosterone. Instead, Cooperstown was a small rectangular patch of asphalt, sidewalk, and parking meters furnished with a couple of vintage trolley cars and what was once a Woolworth's. No massive crowds awaited us within the hall's unassuming brick exterior, though the building was well visited that day, entirely by men: contingents of college dudes; fledgling fathers shepherding their young sons; loners with oversize earphones wrapped around their heads, probably listening to baseball games while they ogled baseball artifacts in the baseball shrine to baseball's greatness. Everyone we saw was wearing at least one article of paraphernalia supporting his favorite team; I had dressed in a T-shirt with the logo for Metroid, a 1980s-era Nintendo game, and I wasn't the least bit out of place. The whole operation was not dedicated to preservation so much as to taxidermy; the spirit of the sport did not reside there so much as it stuck like a bug on flypaper.

All the relics you would expect to see were there, ripped from their familiar contexts: the balls that were hit or missed when records were established, the bats used to wallop them, the gloves that caught them, and the batting helmets they ricocheted off. Some patrons stood with silent reverence at the exhibits, and others took futile photographs through glass display cases—trying to capture images of artifacts that represented long-ago acts and the men who achieved them—of caps and mitts and locker room doors. How far could the adulation go? I wandered the grounds with all the curiosity of a baseball fan who, upon hearing the news that the old Yankee Stadium was to be razed, mourned only for the loss of the rare concession stands that served chicken fingers with French fries.

My father appreciated these items more but enjoyed the trip less. He had been having trouble with his knees, locked in a vicious cycle where his arthritis was making it impossible to exercise regularly, which in turn exacerbated the arthritis and the muscular atrophy, none of which was conducive to a day of walking and standing around looking at sports memorabilia. He lagged behind me and sometimes skipped entire rooms when the pain was too great. When I forged ahead, I could still hear him huffing and puffing, the cadence of his voice rising and falling as he cajoled a passerby or an off-duty tour guide into a casual conversation that soon became a one-way rant about baseball or fatherhood or the fur business. I could hear him slapping his shorts or the sides of his legs to emphasize some unheard point, each one driving some pinprick of irritation deeper into my skin.

That I could not reproduce the physical feats of the men commemorated in this building, could not even play the game they perfected or any other like it, could barely identify who many of its greatest heroes were or what teams they had played for, seemed to me largely the fault of one man. Sure, he had bought me a few bats and gloves in his time, even offered to take me to the park every once in a while to throw a ball around, but by then I was already too set in my ways—too entranced by videogames and television screens and the sedentary satisfaction of sitting at home doing nothing. Even if he could not teach me to play sports, he could have shown me how to talk about them competently, so that the language of earned-run averages, slugging percentages, and fielders' choices that all my friends seemed to speak fluently by third grade did not haunt me like a foreign tongue for the rest of my life. Even now, when he was presented with a belated opportunity to induct me into this most essential masculine tradition, what was he doing? Talking to other people and struggling with his own physical malady.

When we reached the gallery where the Hall of Fame players are honored with vaguely funereal plaques, my father was in too much pain to walk. He sat on a bench, never rising to inspect a single tablet or to see if any of his own boyhood heroes were immortalized here. As he sat down, and when he at last rose to leave the room, he announced, "They ought to put me in the Hall of Fame." With this repeated declaration of endurance, our trip came to an end.

On our drive out of Cooperstown, my father noticed a few signs for a concert, a rare joint appearance by Bob Dylan and Willie Nelson at the local minor-league baseball park, scheduled for later that night. "You wanna go?" my father asked sincerely. We easily could have done it and were already in the right place. We'd just have to get ourselves a pair of tickets and kill a few more hours in Cooperstown. But how would we pass the time? Where could we go that wouldn't require my father to stand and walk? How would he behave at the concert? What if he couldn't understand Dylan? How would he react when Willie used his set to protest the war in Iraq? What if someone offered us a joint? What if I wanted to smoke it? What if *he* wanted to smoke it?

"Nah, that's okay," I said. "I gotta be back in the city tonight."

Somewhere between Cooperstown and Monticello, we stopped to eat at a barbecue stand, a Southern-style restaurant that served its food on long sheets of brown paper. No one preserved my grease-stained paper or rib bones, picked clean of every last morsel of meat. But I came away feeling that I, too, deserved a place in somebody's hall of fame.

VI. The End

Another Saturday morning began with my usual pre-therapy ritual. I was in the lobby of the institute, making steady progress at my crossword puzzle and my bagel, waiting for my father to arrive. Lately, we had been asking Rebecca when we would know it was time to conclude our therapy for good; my father had become so enamored with the process that he had begun evangelizing to his friends about it. He had recently told me about a conversation he'd had with a childhood friend, in which the friend confessed that he'd had a falling-out with his own son, who was about my age. "I told him he should go to his son and get him to go into therapy with him," my father told me with proud, resolute faith.

"Dad," I said, "don't you think we should worry about ourselves first?"

My bagel and my crossword puzzle were complete, and it was nearly time for our session to start, but my father was missing. My cellphone began to ring—and it was him; from the background noise, I could tell he was in his car, which meant he was still several minutes away, and I was instantly anxious. Rebecca had warned him before about being late to our appointments; she had told him that she would not let meetings run long to make up for late starts.

"David," he said over the phone, "I can't remember where the institute is. Can you tell me how to get there?"

"What?" I said, making no effort to stifle an angry laugh. "Are you kidding me?" I realized right away this was the wrong way to respond.

"No, I'm not kidding," he answered. "Can you just give me the goddamn directions?"

"It's in the same place it's been every Saturday morning you've come to it for the last year," I said. I gave him the address and flipped my phone shut.

When my father walked through the front door a few minutes later, his face was flushed and his breath was short. I had to remind myself these were symptoms of his garden-variety anger and nothing worse. "I don't understand why you had to talk to me like that," he said.

When we took our seats in front of Rebecca, the morning's incident was the first and only thing my father wanted to discuss. "Why does he have to be so snide about it?" he said to the room, finding no apparent difficulty in talking about me as if I weren't present. "Why can't he just give me the directions and tell me how to get here?"

"Dad," I said, "this isn't what the therapy process is supposed to be for. If we're going to use every session to debate whatever petty argument of the day, how are we ever going to get to the stuff that's really important?"

"You know," he said, continuing his train of thought, "he has always been a willful child. Even when he was a little boy. Did you know that when he was growing up, I'd be driving in my car, and he'd be sitting in the backseat, and he would lean up to the front to change the radio stations? I'm the one who's driving, and he's the one choosing the stations! Nothing has changed."

"Dad," I said, "I was six years old when that happened. Maybe seven. I can't account for what I did when I was just a kid. I'm not that person anymore."

"Look," my father said, "right now you can't understand what I'm talking about, because you are the son, and I'm the father. But someday, when you have kids of your own and you are the father, you'll know what I meant today."

"Oh my God," I said, looking to Rebecca for any sign of sympathy or consolation. "Is that not the ultimate cop-out? How am I even supposed to respond to that?"

"Hold on, hold on, hold on," Rebecca said in her quiet voice, holding up her hands. "Let's stop this for a second and sort it out. David, what I'm hearing from you is that you want your father to stop criticizing you for things you did a long time ago, in your past, and to start seeing you as an adult. Is that right?"

I murmured a grumble of assent.

"And Mr. Iss-i-koff," she added, "what I'm hearing from you is that you want David to recognize that you've got a perspective he cannot appreciate yet, that there are certain things he won't understand until he becomes a father himself. Is that right?"

"It's interesting that you bring that up," my father replied. "Becky, is your father still alive? What's your relationship like with him?"

Rebecca was startled by his nonanswer. "I'm . . . not sure how that's relevant," she answered. Her attempt at authority was unconvincing.

"Because I wonder if you would ever consider going into therapy with your father," he said. "I think you both might benefit from it."

"What does this have to do with anything?" I said. "We're not here to work the refs, Dad. To debate the moderators. It's not getting us anywhere."

"I'm not allowed to ask Becky about her own father?" he asked.

"Dad, you just suggested that *our* therapist go into therapy."

"No, I didn't."

"You did."

"You don't believe me?" My father began to eye the video camera that had silently and without acknowledgment been recording all of our sessions. "Here," he said, "give me the videotape and
we'll play it back. I'll show you what I said."

I could see him preparing to get out of the chair. He was really
going to do it. "Dad," I said, "that's not what it's for."

"Hey," he said, "that's *me* on there. Those are *my* words. I'm not
allowed to play it back?"

Rebecca interceded. "We're not playing the tape back," she
said. "And really, Mr. Iss-i-koff, let's leave my life out of this."

"I thought this was supposed to be a place where we could talk
about whatever we wanted to talk about," my father said. "Well,
this is what I want to talk about."

"Even if it comes at the cost of alienating everyone in this
room?" I asked.

"David," my father said, "I'm sixty-five years old. I'm pretty
much fixed in my ways at this point. I'm not going to censor myself. I'm not going to change my basic nature for you or for anybody."

"So then," I said, "what was the point of any of this? Why
did you ever agree to come to therapy if you never had any intention of coming out of this thing any different than when you
started?"

And— Wait a second, holy shit, now I remember. I finally remember those twelve horrible words, that one stupid, simple
rhyme that proved to me the whole project was lost. He put his
hand on mine, turned to me, spoke my name, and said:

A man convinced against his will
Is of the same opinion still

"Really?" I said. "So that's your answer? That's it? What the fuck is that?" It might have been the first swearword I'd used in a year's worth of sessions.

"Hey," my father answered, "you can't talk to me like that. In here, we may be peers, but you have to understand something: I'm your father, not your friend."

The funny thing is, I knew exactly what he meant. But all at once everything dropped: the air dropped out of my lungs, the floor dropped out of the room. My heart and my stomach dropped out of my chest, and the clouds dropped out of the sky. I knew how to hear those words so they sounded sane and rational, and I knew how to construe them to sound like the meanest thing he'd ever said to me sober. And in that moment I also knew which way I wanted to interpret them.

The whole process had been revealed as a worthless sham. Maybe I couldn't fight my father with words, but if I didn't give him any words to work with, he would have nothing to fight against. I slumped in my chair, lowered my head, and resolved to myself that I wouldn't speak again for the rest of the session.

My tacit vow had startlingly little effect on the trajectory of the remaining conversation. Words whizzed by; my father reiterated his assertion that I was an exceedingly prompt son while my sister was never on time, and that my sister spent all her money while I saved half of what I made. He retold the anecdote about his friend who had told him of a desire to see his son have sex with his wife; and he repeated the story of discovering his father's glass eye and my grandfather weeping that were it not for his handicap, he could have been president.

Then, mercifully, we ran out of time. I can't be sure, but I doubt Rebecca ended the session with any remark more conclusive or profound than "See you next week."

My pledge of silence continued during the traditional post-therapy diner lunch, but it did not stop my father from conducting a conversation with himself.

"Did you see the game last night?" he asked. "You know, the problem with Torre is that he just wants to prove how right he is. The genius. Always has to meddle. He will not let these guys pitch—will not let them pitch. I say, if you're going to bring a guy in as a reliever, let the man pitch. Let him face a few batters, notch a few outs, build up his confidence. This one's always ready to pull out his pitcher over one bad pitch. Joe Torre the genius. He's no genius, I say."

And then: "You want to know how crazy your mother is? She's pulling the car out of the garage the other day, and she scrapes the whole side of the car along the wall of the garage. Instead of backing out slowly, she has to peel out all at once—she hears the sound of the metal scraping against her car, and she tries to accelerate even faster. It's like I always tell her, 'Maddy, if you're not sure which way the car is going to go, just go slowly.' "

And then: "I gotta say, David, I'm pretty happy with my life up in the mountains. A lot of people say they like warm weather all year round, but me, I like the seasons. I like it when the sun goes down earlier in the day and the air gets colder. I like that things should be cyclical. It lets me know I'm alive. And that's why I could never move to Florida."

I hadn't spoken a word since ordering my club sandwich. At last my father noticed that I wasn't acknowledging his monologues. "Well," he said, "aren't you going to say anything?"

"No," I said, breaking my vow. "Not until you apologize."

"What did I do?"

"You *know* what you said in there."

"David," he said gently, "I thought we had an agreement—what we say in there, we leave in there. We don't take it out here."

"I know you said you wanted an arrangement like that, but I don't remember actually agreeing to it. I don't know that I can abide by it. I can't flip a switch and be two different people. I can't just forget what you said now that I know your mind."

As my father had said to me before, he said again, "We've got to find a way to talk to each other in there. We've got to find a way to signal to each other when one of us is hurting the other one's feelings."

"Dad," I said, "what do you think this has all been about? You *already* hurt my feelings. I don't know what more you could say to hurt them worse. And I don't know that I can hear you say anything like that again."

"I'm sorry," he said, apologizing not for what he had already said but for what he was about to say. "Because I've got to be able to feel I can say whatever I want in that room. I can't censor myself at this age. I'm too far along and too set in my ways."

We finished our lunch quickly and quietly, and he still needed directions from me to drive me home.

Our next two sessions had to be postponed because my father was traveling one weekend, and the next was the Thanksgiving holiday. We had told Rebecca that we would be in contact with her when we were ready to schedule our next appointment. But we never did. One Saturday passed, and then another, and our newly inert routine was cemented. Not once did my father ask me when our therapy schedule might resume.

One morning during the week, when I was working in my office, I got a call from Rebecca. Over the phone, her voice sounded smaller and more distant. "Have you decided when you'll be coming back?" she asked. "I think we still have a few things that we need to work on."

I answered her the same way I would have a publicist who was trying to push a story I wasn't interested in, or a pollster trying to get me to take part in a telephone survey. "There's, ah, a couple things I just need to sort out with my dad," I said. "As soon as I do, I'll get back to you." It was the last thing I ever said to her, and I doubt she bought it.

CHAPTER 7

Here's a story from my adolescence in suburban exile. One afternoon I returned home from a full day of school where I had said nothing to anyone, in preparation for another of the routine afternoon naps that passed the time until the evening, and I found that my parents were already back from work. Their presence in the house before sundown was generally a bad omen: it meant that my father had been pulled away from what he most wanted to be doing, which was yelling into the phone and selling fur.

Earlier that morning they had left for work separately, my mother in her car and my father in his, and by the time he arrived at his office, he could no longer remember how he got there. He could not mentally retrace the uncomplicated route he drove every day of the week—the Palisades Parkway to the George Washington Bridge to the West Side Highway—and could not even recall sitting behind the wheel of his automobile, tapping its pedals with his feet to make it stop or go. He knew his name, where he worked, and who his wife was, but by the time she had driven him back, he had already forgotten how that happened, too.

He could still walk upright and speak clearly, and his personality and sense of humor were in no way altered, but he could not remember anything that had happened to him over five minutes ago. He would notice the group of gardeners working on our front lawn and jokingly ask, "Who are those guys? Mommy's boyfriends?" Then he would resume reading the same page of the newspaper he had been working on all afternoon before once again noticing the gardeners and asking, "Who are those guys? Mommy's boyfriends?"

Transient global amnesia, my mother was told over the telephone later, was what my father was most likely suffering from: a temporary condition lasting no more than a day, in which his long-term memory was unaffected but his short-term memory was impaired. It was explained that this was in no way a threat to his life and would shortly resolve itself without treatment, which it did, but watching him under its weak influence was as excruciating as seeing him suffer through a deadly illness—at least we would have to imagine; to this point, my sister and I had never seen him confined to a hospital bed or stricken with any ailment more severe than bronchitis. For the rest of the day, until he went to bed, my father sat at the kitchen table with the same simple grin, unaware there was anything wrong with him, able to read the distressed expressions on the faces of his family but incapable of recognizing that he was the one who was causing the distress.

Here's another story. On a winter night some months later, my father was driving on an icy patch of road near our home when he lost control of his car and wiped out on a highway divider. His car was completely wrecked, but somehow he emerged from the accident unharmed. A policeman who examined my father at the scene found him disoriented and slightly incoherent and suggested that he see a doctor, believing he may have suffered a stroke during or just before the crash. Actually, he was high on cocaine.

I was thinking about these incidents several years later, as I made the drive to reach my father in his modest house in the Catskills. Having failed at what was supposed to be a fairly conventional and time-tested method of reconciling two occasionally estranged family members, I decided I would try a strategy of my own devising.

I was going to sit my father down and make him tell me his life story. All of it, in as much unexpurgated detail as he could remember, with a special emphasis on his cocaine addiction, a history that stretched back even further than his history with me; which began casually long before my existence was even contemplated; which reached its frenzied, catastrophic zenith with eerie synchronicity right around the time I was born; and which continued for years and years and *years*—and then ended at a moment that was difficult to pinpoint precisely, for reasons I was still not completely sure I understood.

I thought that in hearing this story told to me and diligently writing it down, I could turn it into a coherent narrative. As I learned the many details of his life I did not know; heard him retell the tales he had told on a thousand previous occasions for their thousand and first time; had him correct all the inaccuracies I had mistakenly propagated in my erroneous accounts of these episodes; dispelled my mythologies; and exposed my biases, I thought I might be able to show my father a side of himself he did not realize he possessed. Maybe I could show him how close we had been in the times when we seemed furthest apart. Only, to compile this account, I had to start with a man whose own memory could not be trusted, who could lie to your face with a smile whether he realized he was doing it or not.

Traveling to my father in the Catskills is like passing through a ripple in time. From my own unexceptional Manhattan dwelling, the hundred-mile trip upstate is almost entirely confined to highways, until I exit onto a two-lane access road where the unrelenting advancement of the years yields for its most faithful traveler, age sixty-nine, and appears to run backward from the perspective of the son half his age. On my left-hand side, I pass proud monuments to my father's past, still vital and only gently touched, if at all, by the progress of the present day: colonies of weather-beaten but sturdy bungalows, nearly identical to those where he spent his childhood summers, and where I later spent mine; the horse-racing track that recently welcomed its first supply of slot machines. From my right-hand window, I watch symbols of ambiguous potentiality recede from view: wide green fields forlornly planted with for-sale signs; dirt paths that branch off into countless unpaved tributaries, none of which I have attempted to explore to their unknown ends.

The route winds around the lake where my mother once photographed me at age six, surrounded by water and clinging to my father's towering legs for support; beyond the wooden sign advertising the summer vacation properties where my parents can now be found year-round, even in winter; and finally, to row upon row of undifferentiated cedar-colored cottages, one of which shelters my father and mother, their dog, their menagerie of ceramic ducks, and their collection of throw pillows stitched with mottoes like EAT, SLEEP, FISH and OLD FRIENDS ARE THE BEST FRIENDS. It's a long way to go to enjoy the privilege of believing your life is no different from anyone else's.

Other than the fear that I would not get home from my trip in time for a Sunday-night episode of *The Simpsons*, I had no trepidation about asking my father to reveal all the secrets and details of his life in a single weekend. Although I had not learned about his addiction until I was eight, from that moment on, there was no part of his personal history that my father ever kept secret from me. He may not be proud of the life he previously led, I thought, but nor would he ever deny how he led it. In fact—and you will simply have to take my word on this—were you to spend no more than five minutes in my father's company, he would probably confess as much to you, followed by some randomly selected anecdote from his substance-abuse highlight reel. The last time I had visited my parents, bringing Amy upstate with me so she could see their home, we were all eating bagels at the dinner table when my father spontaneously decided to tell us the decades-old story of the time a group of his business associates introduced him to freebase cocaine. "We were all in a circle," he recounted, "and when you were done, you were supposed to pass it to the guy sitting next to you. And by the time *he* was done, you already wanted it back."

When I had proposed this biographical project to my father several months before, he agreed without hesitation, but in the days leading up to this visit, he was growing increasingly anxious. "What if I don't have any interesting stories to tell you?" he asked. "What if I can't remember all the details so well? How am I going to know which parts of my life I should focus on? Do you want to know only about the drugs, or should I just cover everything? Because there's a lot of tough stuff in there."

"You don't have to worry about any of it," I told him. "Let me be the one to figure out how everything fits together. I'll ask the questions, and you answer them. All you have to do is be yourself. I know you can do that."

He was fully in character when I arrived that morning, still dressed in yesterday's underwear clinging to his sweaty skin, spread across his living room couch, where he had spent the morning nodding off to the din of barking political commentators on a wide-screen television.

"How are you feeling?" I asked him.

"Still living," came the reply. As I strode into his living room, he lifted himself off his couch to embrace me, leaving behind the imprint of his body on the couch. "How do I look?" the man of the house asked. "Do I look like a porcupine?"

There was a single word that best described him, a word I had long resisted but which I begrudgingly accepted, and that word was "old." For years, I could conveniently regard him as fat, which he genuinely used to be, as much as 250 or 300 pounds at his 1990s-era peak. Then he lost over a hundred pounds in a single year, using a punishing exercise regimen I never would have predicted he would maintain so diligently. After he lost all that weight, the physical characteristic that most defined him was either—take your pick—the assemblage of short, staccato quills of silver hair that poked up from his scalp like the snow-glossed blades of grass outside, or a thin crimson scar underneath his left eye, the obstinate reminder of a minor surgical operation that he never bothered to have closed up.

It was not just his newly thin face, with its once flattened-out features consolidated and hardened, the skin taut and angular where it used to be paunchy, that was no longer immediately identifiable to me. It was the complete person, suddenly mindful of his health, determined that his survival on this planet be allowed to continue as long as possible, and aware that he himself might play some role in his own preservation. It was the man who seemed to be perfectly comfortable with his advancing age, who appeared to have all the competing spheres of his universe in harmonious balance, and who, in reverent tones, repeatedly declared to me in conversation after conversation that he had never felt so at ease in all his life.

The feeling that his expressions of contentment stirred in me was not relief but irritation. I knew I should be pleased that he had, over a period of decades, meandered his way to inner peace, and grateful that, as his heir, I might be genetically predisposed to achieving the same. But when I was being truthful with myself, I caught myself thinking he simply didn't deserve to live a life so blissfully free of suffering. I felt all of this every time he so much as picked up the phone to ask me if I'd caught the Yankees game or if I'd heard from my sister lately.

My mother was seated at a nearby breakfast table, eating cereal. "He was up all night playing with the computer," she explained without looking up from her bowl.

Swatting away my mother's remark as if it were a fly, my father led me into his private den. It was here that his recently acquired top-of-the-line PC resided—the one he had compulsively upgraded with all manner of anti-virus software and anti-spyware detection programs, memory boards, hard drives, and video capture cards. His latest technological lust object was the scanner he used to digitize the contents of his photo albums. By day he organized these files into virtual portfolios, and by night he ruminated over faded photographs of himself from his childhood, pictures of my mother in the earliest years of their marriage, when they still went on vacations, pictures of me and my sister when we crawled on our knees and sucked on pacifiers—even pictures he had taken of other people's children at the bungalow colony whose lake he fished on during the summer. If it was fragile and innocent and would someday be gone, rest assured that my father had recorded it somewhere.

Surrounded by these implements that offered him instanta-
neous, on-demand, and perpetual evocations of his past, we sat
across from each other in plastic folding chairs; I had a legal pad
and a pen in my lap. "Okay," my father said, "where do you want to
start?"

We started at the beginning, in 1940, in the Bronx neighborhood of Pelham Parkway, in the apartment building at 2167
Cruger Avenue where my father was raised and lived until he was
sixteen. What he remembered most about the neighborhood was
how closely knit families were in those days: how his friends
(who called him Gerry) lived not only with their parents (who
called him Gerald) but with aunts, uncles, grandparents, and
anyone else who shared their last names whom they could fit into
a three-room tenement. As he enumerated each of his surviving
friends, he dutifully recited the apartment number, public
school, and ultimate location of retirement, whether to Long Island, Florida, or Aspen; for the elders, the medical condition that
led to deaths.

His other favorite memory from this formative era was throwing up on his walk to school every single day. It was a story I could
easily reconcile with the man my father became—oblivious of
punctuality, unnerved by the thought of being asked questions he
was unprepared to answer, and endlessly fearful of the unknown.
It was much harder for me to comprehend how that timid little
schoolboy matured into a young man who had graduated high
school by the age of sixteen and who, that following summer, was
attending college in New Orleans, playing cards and throwing
dice in its backroom gambling parlors; who, by age twenty-one,
had joined his father in the family fur business and, within twelve
months, was turning greater profits than in any year when my
grandfather ran it alone.

He had flunked out of college twice (or possibly three times, he couldn't remember), taken a job at a local bank, and threatened to enlist in the Merchant Marine before my grandfather invited him to join the business. The great irony was that this was what my father had wanted to do all along, but he was too embarrassed or too weak to raise the issue with my grandfather. Until then, "I had no life, no direction," my father had explained to me. "I could never ask for what I wanted. I probably wouldn't have gotten it. Or maybe I would.

"I was always striving to get somewhere," my father said. "Only there ain't nothing out there."

He rarely exhibited these qualities now, but after a couple of years of dealing fur with my grandfather, my father had a sense of purpose, he had a steady income, and most significantly, he had confidence.

Case in point: at age twenty, in the years before fur, my father had been hanging out at the Playdrome Bowling Center in the Bronx, now demolished, when he first laid eyes on Madelin Klugman, a fifteen-year-old brunette whom he swears still possesses, at age sixty-four, the same cherubic face she had when she was seven. He became instantly smitten with her but was too shy to approach her. Three years later, post-fur, he received a hot tip from his cousin Heshie that she had just broken up with her boyfriend, Morty Mandelbaum, and this was his chance to make a move.

(Who was Morty Mandelbaum, by the way? Why, the very same dope fiend with whom my father had been arrested for smoking marijuana on a Parkchester rooftop the previous year. Why had she broken up with him? Because late one night he had driven her out to a seedy neighborhood and left her in the car while he went to buy pot. Did she know at the time that my father had been busted with him under similar circumstances? "Probably not," said the old dad.)

On Cousin Heshie's recommendation, my father, with uncharacteristic poise and promptness, phoned up his teenage crush and asked for a date, and when she said she was too busy to meet with him that week, he called her a second time and she invited him to meet her at a friend's apartment in Manhattan. From that point on, my father said, "I saw her every night until I married her. Except when I was out late playing cards."

In the itinerary of twists and turns that comprised my father's life, maybe this one was the most significant. To this point he had yearned with every ounce of strength and desire he possessed for love: to have love in his life and to have love radiated back to him as intensely as he projected it. Now he had found it, with a woman who, by his own estimation, seemed hopelessly beyond his grasp, and not only was the love good and fulfilling for its own sake, but he found that it amplified all the hidden qualities within him that he had been forced to bring to the surface in order to win it. Having love in his life affirmed his ambition; it bolstered his confidence; it broadened his sense of personal capability; and it imbued him with a previously unknown sense of courage.

My parents were married in 1965, and I like to imagine the decade that followed as their Martin Scorsese years—a montage set to a soundtrack of hit AM-radio rock singles, with each smash cut in the sequence signifying another rung ascended on the socioeconomic ladder. Begin with their brief post-honeymoon period as tenants of the guest bedroom of my father's parents' apartment in Bronxville (set to the Chiffons' "Sweet Talkin' Guy"); cut to their first real home in Yonkers (Love Affair's "Everlasting Love"); cut to their Manhattan high-rise (Elton John's

"Tiny Dancer"); cut to their weekend house in New Jersey (the Rolling Stones' "Wild Horses"). There were cars, there were parties, there were vacations in Mexico, and there were, of course, fur coats. There was money to spare, and after ten years, there was a baby on the way.

Also, there were drugs. Despite my father's previous experiences and my mother's earlier objections, they inhaled pot as if it were oxygen: they smoked it with their other newly married friends, smoked it with their lawyer and stockbroker pals on their lunch breaks, drove all the way to New Hope, Pennsylvania, to smoke it outdoors, sorted it and deseeded it on album covers, and smoked it in the privacy of their own home. They were not hippies or anti-establishment types, or anti-anything, for that matter—just a couple of newly independent young adults for whom marijuana seemed like the latest innovation in their rapidly evolving middle-class ethos, a novelty whose lifestyle benefits would eventually become as indispensable and as commonplace as food processors and permanent-press fabric.

If you're the sort of armchair rebel whose mouth instinctively folds into a smirk when you hear an authority figure describe marijuana as a gateway drug, consider what happened next. For years my unstylish parents, a furrier and a garment worker, had been toiling by tradition in midtown Manhattan's fashion district, a neighborhood of co-existing squalor and sophistication, mixing it up with some very worldly people. Through one of my mother's friends, a young clothing designer my father referred to as "a real fruit fly," they were invited to a party where they were introduced to another new recreational product that was becoming popular with their young urban demographic, this one called cocaine.

My father tried it out, seemed to like it, and upon subsequent samplings at later parties, discovered that he truly enjoyed it. It allowed him to let go of his social anxieties, to say things that he believed in his heart but that his conscious mind wouldn't allow him to enunciate, and to feel sexually emboldened around my mother. Unlike pot, which altered his consciousness to a point that he could no longer be sure was his own, cocaine seemed to reach a genuine part of himself that was always there but which he could not otherwise set free.

On a later trip to Florida, my father similarly talked himself into a group of young pilots and their girlfriends. This new set of thrill-seeking companions taught him how to parachute out of a plane, and they helped him mainline cocaine by cooking it up and injecting it directly into his bloodstream. The first time they tied him in to the intravenous gear, they strictly warned my father that they were going to allow him to do it only once. Of course, he liked the experience so much that he immediately wanted to do it again. *No,* they reminded him. *Remember, we said only once.*

They did, however, help him purchase a pound of solid co-caine, which rode shotgun with him when he drove home to New York. Not knowing what to do with such a large quantity of the drug, my father hid a portion of it in the freezer, believing this would somehow keep it fresh, and then divided the remaining amount into smaller bags of one ounce each, which he concealed in tiny slits he cut into the couch in his living room. It was around this time, my father would later conclude, that he officially crossed the threshold from the dimly lit, curtains-drawn den of the casual drug user to the night-dark, windowless back room of the true addict. He ran a reasonably successful fur business and had a fairly happy marriage, but now he had found something he could devote himself to completely and love with all his heart. One year later, I was born.

My mother started taking my father to psychiatrists for his drug problem during my infancy; by that point his cocaine use was so pervasive and all-encompassing that there was no part of our family history that was not in some way built on its shifting, powdery foundation. He was getting high so often that he was staying awake for days at a time and having paranoid delusions that unknown assailants were climbing ropes up the side of our apartment building, preparing to enter through the windows and take him away. During one such panic attack, he dashed out of our apartment dressed in nothing more than a T-shirt and a pair of jogging shorts; he ran all the way to a nearby Hilton hotel, where he checked in to a room and waited for the hallucination to subside.

("And I'm using, and I'm using," my father would later explain to me. "How come nobody threw a net over me?")

At my mother's request—probably more like her insistence, under pain of death or nighttime castration—my father went with her to meet a psychiatrist named Dr. Nichols at his private practice in the East Village. After he considered the same evidence I just recounted, the delusions and the assailants and the Hilton hotel, Dr. Nichols delivered the same assessment that every other friend, casual acquaintance, and passerby on the street had been offering my father: he needed to check in to a hospital and get treated for his addiction. Otherwise, said Dr. Nichols, "You're headed for big trouble."

How seriously did my parents take Dr. Nichols's diagnosis? Seriously enough to compose a song about it. It was an original number that was later sung to me in a different context, called "Big Trouble," set to the tune of the hit Jimmy Dean song "Big Bad John" and whose complete lyrics ran as follows:

Big trouble
Big bad trouble

My father's symptoms did not get better of their own accord. He became emboldened and even more open about his habits. At the Friday-night dinners where he gathered with his parents, he sneaked off to the bathroom to get high. He was making so much money from his fur business and buying so much coke that, in those instances when he determined that his unseen captors were coming for him, he could easily afford to flush a half pound of the drug down the toilet and replace it later.

This was followed by a session with another psychiatrist named Dr. Goldman, who specialized in analytic psychology. Upon entering Dr. Goldman's office, my father declared, "It smells like tuna fish in here." To which Dr. Goldman replied, "What do you think that means?"

My father's private meetings with Dr. Goldman yielded nothing more memorable or lasting than tuna fish, but it was he who wrote the order to have my father committed, which my mother signed and my grandfather dispiritedly seconded. On a night when my sister and I had been given over to our grandmother for safekeeping, my father's visions of a traumatic, violent abduction were realized when the police came banging at his apartment door, stripped him naked and strapped him into a straitjacket, and hijacked him to Bellevue Hospital. He spent the next month there, trying to rationalize with his doctors that he would clean up his act if they'd release him back to his family. He was devoid of companionship save for the transients, schizophrenics, and other hopeless cases who were treated alongside him, and a lone visit from the father who co-signed his commitment papers, who told his haggard, depleted son, "You're still the best-looking guy in here."

Thirty days later, clean and sober, reunited with his wife and young children, and liberated from the fear that he would be ripped away from his loved ones a second time, my father resumed his drug habit. Within months he was institutionalized again, this time by his own volition, at the Long Island Jewish Hospital, a live-in facility that he was free to walk away from at any time. At least one of his fellow patients did that during his stay, skipping out in the middle of the night, but my father fulfilled his commitment to the program, contented by the freedom that came with wearing nothing but a hospital gown all day, by his roommates (including a long-haired guitar player who asked to be called Gandalf), and by the occasional visits from his friends, one of whom presented him with a copy of James Allen's classic tome of new age philosophy, *As a Man Thinketh* (sample aphorism: "Man is always the master, even in his weakest and most abandoned state; but in his weakness and degradation he is the foolish master who misgoverns his 'household' ").

Around this time my father became so proficient and attentive in his drug use that he assembled a personal soundtrack of the music he believed was most compatible with his frame of mind when he was alone and high. I think it says something about my father that his two favorite albums to snort cocaine to were the Spinners' *Greatest Hits* and Emmylou Harris's *Pieces of the Sky*. His choice of the Spinners I can almost understand, even if it is the sort of record I could never imagine him listening to while sober; it has a certain soothing quality that's exacerbated when one's senses are chemically attuned to the deep, rich vocals and pulsating bass lines.

The Emmylou Harris selection I find more surprising, even for a lifelong country-music fan like my father. To a completely sober

listener, Harris's sweet, piercing voice already possesses sufficient intensity to sweep your legs out from under you; how she
must sound to a dedicated substance abuser when she applies
that same sonorous power to a laid-back honky-tonk number
like "Too Far Gone," its metaphoric suggestions of loss and dependency amplified by a genuine act of debasement taking place
as it plays, is too terribly resonant for me to contemplate. There
are biblical references throughout the album, which always seem
more compelling, somehow, when you're intoxicated, and a
vague, recurring theme of personal salvation. Strongest of all are
the lyrics to "Boulder to Birmingham." I wonder if my father
appreciated the song because Harris wrote it for a friend, Gram
Parsons, whom she lost to substance abuse, or because its descriptions of scenes of natural devastation perfectly mirrored my
father's mental state as he was listening to it:

I was in the wilderness and the canyon was on fire
And I stood on the mountain in the night and I watched it burn

It is hard for me to play *Pieces of the Sky* now and not hear it as
anything other than a purgative, a record my father used to extract
his sadness and to help him shape and guide it. It is a sad man indeed who gets stoned to make himself feel sadder.

Everywhere my father and I looked at the fabric of his life,
without looking very hard at all, we found the stain of cocaine
residue. Did I know, he told me, that just to prove to his own
mother that he was *not* hopelessly addicted to the drug, he once
shot up in front of her while she watched, aghast? Then he
offered her the needle and asked if she'd like to try it for herself.
("I was only surprised," he says later, "that she couldn't see the
benefit.")

But wait—wait—wait—"I'm going to throw this one at you," said my father, poking me firmly on the shoulder with his index finger, "see how you handle this": did I know that my father was high at my bris? In the apartment I grew up in, surrounded by his family, friends, and closest colleagues, on what should have been the happiest day in his life to that point, he was stoned—so stoned that people who were in attendance not only noticed but still remind him to this day. "I'm surprised they didn't just shoot me," he said.

In a softer, more sincere tone, he added, "Is it any wonder I don't think about these things too much?"

We hadn't even crossed the threshold of the 1980s, and already I could see that there wasn't enough paper in my notepad to fit the astounding and unsettling revelations that were being delivered to me page after page. "Do you want to know only about the drugs, or should I just cover everything?" he had asked me earlier. What the hell's the difference, Dad? Is there anything *but* drugs? Without the drugs, what story would there be?

Maybe this was what my father had been trying to warn me about: not that he was afraid he had nothing to tell me but that what he would reveal to me would be overwhelming. *You wanted honesty? Well, now you got it.* At that moment I honestly wasn't sure I could continue our conversation. Maybe there should be a natural limit to the amount of openness that can exist within a family. Maybe there is such a thing as too much honesty, even between a father and a son.

My father surely sensed in my drooping, defeated body language that I needed a break. "Come here," he said. "I want to show you something." We got up and walked a few feet from his den into a hallway, where he brought me to another of his beloved devices: a digital answering machine. He approached it and, without explanation, pressed the play button, setting loose a string of some fifteen or twenty messages, all left either by me or by my sister, each one beginning with more or less the same words:

"Hi, it's me—"

"Hi, guys, it's me—"

"Hey, 's' me—"

"Hi-*iii*! It's me-*eee*—"

My father wasn't interested in the content of each message, when it was left, or under what circumstances; as soon as he heard the singsong greeting—so perfectly intimate and instantly familiar that his son and daughter long ago gave up the practice of identifying themselves by name—he hit the fast-forward key and skipped to the next one. "Isn't that something?" he said proudly, as if contemplating our college diplomas.

My parents took me out for dinner that night in their sleepy, economically depressed Catskills community, and over French-dip sandwiches and waffle fries, I asked them what had become of my father's cousin Heshie, who had facilitated their first meeting and ultimately their marriage. What was he up to these days? They chuckled, and my father related a story he seemed fairly certain he had told me before. But trust me, had I heard the story previously, I would have remembered it.

Several years ago, my father had been told by his aunt and uncle that Heshie was killed in a car accident. Months elapsed, during which time the aunt and uncle also passed away, and then my father received a mysterious phone call from the FBI. The agent asked my father if he was familiar with certain associates whom Heshie had been seen with before his demise. When my father asked what the man meant, he learned that his aunt and uncle had not been entirely truthful with him. At his death, Heshie had indeed been found in a car, but riddled with bullet wounds, inflicted most likely by the organized criminals for whom he was placing horse-racing bets, and whose winnings he had been less than meticulous about returning to them in their entirety. End of Cousin Heshie and his story.

"Oh," I said. "That's too bad. I would have liked to hear his version of the day you got busted for smoking pot."

"Well," my father said, "I still have my arrest record, if you'd like to see it."

It was like hearing my father tell me that he owned an original signed copy of the Declaration of Independence. Had he been in possession of this sacred parchment all along? The seed that the roots and trunk and branches of his addiction story had grown from—would I soon be holding it in my own trembling hands? "Can I see it?" I asked.

"I suppose so," my father said, "as soon as we finish dinner."

It was all I could think about as I excitedly wolfed down my meal and anxiously discouraged my parents from poring over that last pickle on their dinner plates or ordering one more cup of coffee for the road, as I hastened them back into their car and along the cracked and untended asphalt streets that led us back to their cramped home.

While my parents scavenged their overstuffed abode for the documents, I recited to myself all the events that had followed from my father's notorious arrest: how he spent the night in prison at the Bronx County Courthouse, how he had to be bailed out the following morning by his humiliated mother, who then hired the son of a beloved local rabbi to be the lawyer in his defense. And how, though the case against my father was thrown out over violations of search-and-seizure procedures, he was not allowed to leave the state of New York for a period of time, which meant that instead of spending the summer in New Orleans selling fur with my grandfather, as he'd planned, he'd have to remain in the Bronx, painting apartment buildings with his uncle Hymie. Some years later, when my father got his fateful call to appear in front of a draft board that took notice of the arrest, he was able to manipulate the blot on his record to his advantage, teaching himself for all time that drugs made his life thrilling and worthwhile, and that he was nimble enough to concoct alibis for any danger they might get him into, even if he lacked the foresight to anticipate those dangers.

I clung to these details like a rosary every time my mother or father finished searching an area of the house and returned empty-handed. Would I come this close to glimpsing my birthright only to discover that my parents had unthinkingly chucked it during some long-ago moving process, along with a king's ransom in unused McDonald's coupons and half-melted Hanukkah candles? Finally, my mother announced that she had found the artifact in an old jewelry box I had rummaged through untold times as a child, never knowing the real treasure it possessed.

There was first a typewritten paper arrest record, turned pink with time, which noted that my father "Did have in his possession a quantity of marihuana," and at his arrest, he possessed no scars, marks, or deformities.

Beneath it was attached an old photograph of a young man standing in front of a stark white background, his head crowned by the outline of an absent staple that once held the picture to the typed report, giving him the unfortunate appearance of devil's horns. The young man had an unmistakable look of fear on his face; he clearly knew he had committed an act of wrongdoing for which he was about to be punished—if not by the City of New York, then by a Jewish mother from the Bronx, which was arguably worse. Though the baby-smooth skin and the jet-black hair that

stood a full inch above his scalp, combed and Brylcreemed into
obedience, did not endure, in his adolescent face there was already a chubbiness waiting to emerge, the suggestion of a double
chin that would not fully assert itself for several more years. His
eyes, to the extent that they could be seen behind the glare of
bright lights reflected in the lenses of his thick black glasses, had
a familiar smallness. Viewed from the side in an accompanying
right-profile shot, my father appeared content, but head-on,
he was so visibly uncomfortable with his surroundings and
himself that the beholder cannot help but feel a little ill at ease
himself.

Beneath my father's face, a black clapboard held by an unseen
hand at his shoulder line reported an arrest number, the legend
NYC POLICE, and the date the picture was taken: December 5, 1962.
This meant that my father was twenty-two years old—very nearly
twenty-three—at the time of his arrest, not a teenager, as he always was in his recollections of the event. This made it almost
impossible for the narrative to have unfolded in the way my father
had historically described it: it was highly unlikely that a military
physical would have followed soon after his bust, and even if one
did, there was no conflict our army was engaged in at the time, no
real danger from which my father would have extricated himself
by posing as a drug addict.

"What does this mean?" I asked my father.

"Well," he said, "shows you what I know."

Maybe the only time I had seen my father so unconcerned with
his own discrepancies had been back when he was teaching me
how to drive. When I would get bored or impatient with the minimal speed he allowed me in the high school parking lot, he would
conclude his lessons by letting me take the car out on the highway, where I could park myself in the left-hand lane and put my

foot to the floor, though I never could remember which off-ramp we needed to get ourselves home.

"Are we getting close?" the speed demon would ask his father as cars and signs went whizzing by.

"Don't worry," he said. "You got time."

So I would make no move, and within moments, our required exit would inevitably come bounding over the horizon. "Dad," I would say, hurriedly dodging around the traffic to make our escape, "I thought you told me I had time to change lanes."

"Yeah," he would answer, "but what's time to you, and what's time to me?"

CHAPTER 8

For the all times my father had been institutionalized as punishment for his cocaine habit and all the times he had been sentenced to therapy upon release, there was little he had learned and retained. That is, except for one brief mantra that he'd had repeated to him throughout these occasions, which was: No War Stories. He took that to mean he should never romanticize his drug-fueled escapades, shouldn't exchange the anecdotes like currency with fellow addicts, and shouldn't boast about them to temperate listeners in attempts to burnish his street cred. The retelling of the tales with any emotional affect whatsoever was somehow as terrible as desiring the substances that had given rise to them: a sign that the teachings of his many sobriety support groups had not been properly internalized and a first treacherous step on the road to relapsing.

But were we abiding by the No War Stories rule? So far, my father seemed to believe that he was. What he had told me was neither a plea for forgiveness nor a puffing up of his chest; he wasn't

demeaning or glorifying his drug habit, just reciting things that
had happened to him. But I could sense that he was approaching
his limit: he had given me all that he could, or all that he thought
he was capable of, or all that he could remember while seated in a
folding chair in a Catskills cabin that was totally disconnected
from all the times and locations where the real action had gone
down.

Still, I needed more from him. If he wasn't going to give it to
me willingly, knowingly, I had to find some other way to elicit the
information without his realizing he was giving anything up.
What he needed was context—to be re-embedded where these
events had taken place, reconnected with the people who might
remind him of more of his own history or perhaps even report it
for him. (He could hardly be accused of telling war stories if
someone else was doing the telling.) There was only one way to
accomplish this: we needed to get out into the world, together.

I started by following my father to the latest in an annual series
of high school class reunions he had been attending, organized
by the editors of a newsletter called the *Pelham Parkway Times*.
This was a homegrown publication that the former denizens of
his old Bronx neighborhood supplied with new and vintage
photographs, reminiscences and obituaries, advertisements for
condominiums in Boca Raton, and inspirational messages for
their surviving classmates. (A sampling from one issue: "Think
about this. **You** may not realize it, but it's 100% true. 1. There are
at least two people in this world that **you** would die for. 2. At least
15 people in this world love **you** in some way.")

On the morning of the gathering that would mark the fiftieth
anniversary of my father's graduation, he arrived in Manhattan
to take me to the reunion, driving the same Ford Taurus that
had been my car in college. He was suffering from a variety of

physical ailments; his voice was going hoarse with even minimal exertion; and his back was hurting him badly enough that he asked me to drive him the rest of the trip. "It's not the end of the world," he explained. "It only *feels* like the end of the world."

When we arrived at the Long Island park that was the most convenient meeting point for the maximum number of Bronx expatriates, we could see it was very sparsely attended. My father assured me that when he first began going to these reunions in the 1980s, they drew hundreds if not thousands of his old neighbors; on each tree in the park hung a sign designating a different street from Pelham Parkway—Cruger Avenue, Matthews Avenue, White Plains Road—where former residents would congregate to ask, "You lived here, too?" Today all we could see were lonely trees with unattended signs. "Last man standing gets to drink the champagne," my father said.

From a distance, he was able to identify acquaintances who went by nicknames like Butchie and Cookie and Chickie and Moose; this one was the son of a much despised science teacher, and that one worked as a soda jerk at the old C&R drugstore. He described himself in relation to these people as a shy child, a condition exacerbated by a rapid-advance program that skipped him ahead two grades and his mother's ceaseless refrains of "What are you doing tonight?" Even among the classmates who had pushed past that introversion to become his friends, none today made reference to his history with drugs. Possibly they did not know, or possibly they were willing to allow my father a peace that I still could not permit him, in the same way that he would from time to time notice a certain face in the crowd and identify its bearer to me as having once been an inveterate gambler, or a womanizer, or a drunk, only to stop himself in midremembrance to say, "He grew out of it. So what? No big deal."

An old classmate he disliked walked past us. "See that guy?" he said quietly. "He used to be attractive."

Another of my father's old friends, Robert Nadelman, whose family lived next door to the Itzkoffs—close enough that the two boys constructed a tin-can telephone system that ran between their bedroom windows—reminded me of a tale I had not thought about in years. One morning my grandfather told my father that he would take him and his friends on a fishing trip. When the boys had assembled in the Itzkoff family car, with my grandfather at the wheel and my father in the front passenger seat, my grandfather asked my father, "Where's your hat?" My father realized he had forgotten it and went back to the apartment to retrieve it—at which point my grandfather drove off with my father's young friends in tow.

"I thought your grandfather would just drive around the block," Robert recalled to me, still laughing at the memory, "but he went straight to the lake and took us fishing. I bet your father never forgot his hat again."

As Robert went to mingle elsewhere, I saw that my father had become quite agitated and was starting to pace angrily. "Why did he have to tell that story?" my father muttered. "Why do people always want to remember the bad times? I have nothing but good memories of my childhood. When I look back on my life, it was all—*perfect*."

I asked if he would take me back to his old neighborhood, perhaps as soon as the next weekend. He declined. "It's just too much," he said. "It's a lot to deal with right now. We'll do it eventually, I promise."

Amy and I were living together now, and when I came home that evening and confessed to her what felt like a defeat, she urged my patience.

"He's scared, Dave," she told me, not because she was trying to demean him but because she was trying to get me to see something I could not. "Think about how hard this must be for him, and how frightening. Think about how he doesn't want you to see him this way."

"Amy," I said, "I have seen him in much, much worse states."

"But not like this," she said.

"So what am I supposed to do until he decides he's ready to let me see these parts of his life? Just sit around and wait? That day might never come."

"Well," she said, "you might have to do some of it on your own."

The following Saturday, I wandered into Pelham Parkway alone. From my apartment, the subway ride took an hour and left me on a long stretch of the parkway that would lead me straight to Cruger Avenue. As I walked past recreation centers and single-story homes with gated windows and modestly decorated patios, I was reminded of another anecdote that Robert Nadelman had told at the reunion: at some stage of my father's brief college career, he had driven home with a friend who, upon seeing the neighborhood for the first time, remarked, "Gerry, you never told me you lived in the slums."

What I saw were not slums but dignified old brick tenements, sturdy and well maintained, as immaculate as when my father and his family moved into them. Some had tightly woven metal fences to keep trespassers and handball players out of their alleys; others had stately mock-Tudor roofs, and gardens, and more trees on a single block than you will find in a Manhattan mile. Those who once inhabited the neighborhood might be surprised to learn that its character endured without them, perpetuated by another generation of shirtless boys who leaned out of windows to shout to neighbors in upstairs apartments, women who tossed their losing lottery tickets into garden enclosures, and men who rinsed the dirt from their shoes in stagnant puddles of rainwater.

Turning a corner, I found myself in front of 2167 Cruger Avenue, a Gothic-style building called the Arnold Court. Its archway entrance featured an eerily generative decoration of descending vines that split off into ever more vines, inevitably evoking a family tree. A woman who saw me staring at the arch assumed I lived there myself, so she held the door open for me and let me inside. Standing in the drab, cavernous lobby, I could see the door that would have led into the old Itzkoff apartment, a 450-square-foot domicile where my grandparents slept on a foldout couch in the living room while my father and his brother and sister shared its only bedroom. I could also see a handwritten sign on the door from the current tenant:

Worker, I had an emergency at work, please come back tomorrow.

I began to feel like I was intruding upon something I was never meant to see this way—I thought for some reason about the Old Testament proscription that forbade exposing the nakedness of a parent—and I decided I would explore no more today.

In a few weeks my father and I reunited at Newark Airport. We had never traveled together by plane as adults, and since he did not allow himself to take vacations, he flew only when it meant he had to be at the funeral of an out-of-town former client. On this occasion we were not headed anywhere nearly as foreboding, even though he sardonically stopped to point out the location of every emergency respirator we passed in the terminal, as if to say, *You may not need to know this now, but pay attention for later.*

We were on our way to Toronto, where our exploration of my father's history would bring us to a fur auction that he used to participate in regularly but had stopped visiting years ago. He still received the catalogs from the organization that was conducting the sale, the North American Fur Auctions, which dated back to 1670, making it older than the United States itself. I liked this bit of trivia because it seemed to confirm the epochal significance that the fur business held for the Itzkoff family.

It was the industry that gave them their foothold in this country—the one that my great-grandfather Morris, my great-uncles Louis, Nathan, and Hymie, and my grandfather Bob turned to after the family arrived from Russia in the early 1900s after failing to find work in New York and struggling to run a subsistence farm in Alabama, where the local population afforded them about as much respect as the slaves freed a half century prior. When the family returned to New York a few years later, it was the fur business that welcomed them back with neither reprimand nor apology, where Morris Itzkoff found employment as a tailor, and where each of his sons established his own shop in the raw-skin trade. Their new businesses endured so well and so long that each man was able to hand them down to their sons a generation later; the point where the fathers' prosperity had peaked was where their children's would begin.

In the years I had known my grandfather, who was among the first members of his family to be born in America and who died just before I turned thirteen, I always thought of him as a rugged man who enjoyed his horse races and a good cigar—the embodiment of American mobility fused with two-handed Eastern European self-sufficiency. But it wasn't until he brought my father into his firm that the operation really began to thrive: over four decades after the fact, my father could still recount precisely that in the year when my grandfather made him a 25 percent partner, the company had assets totaling thirty thousand dollars, mostly in fur and outstanding debts. By the following year, they were making more money than my father could keep track of—enough that he was able to pay for his first car, a 1964 Corvair convertible, entirely in cash. My father had turned out to be even more aggressive than his father, and while Itzkoff the elder spent most of the calendar year in New Orleans, buying up fur and resisting his son's exhortations to purchase even more of it, Itzkoff the younger remained behind in New York, selling the pelts to any and every trader in Manhattan who would take them.

The wizened old fur merchants of my grandfather's generation took a particular liking to my father; they appreciated his youthful energy and his attentiveness, and they took him out to lunches and offered him their counsel even though he was technically their competitor. Those men were long gone, but my father never forgot their faces or their names and never stopped repeating aloud the lessons they had taught him.

What he could not remember quite as easily was the location of the auction. After we checked in to our room at a highway-strip hotel not far from the airport, I followed him across eight lanes of traffic to the campus of a corporate mall. What had caught his attention there was a tall clay-colored building that clearly bore the letters and logo of the HSBC bank, but which he decided was the headquarters of a commercial operation called the Hudson's Bay Company. After several rings of a buzzer outside the building's deserted lobby yielded no reply, my father remained as certain as ever that the auction was taking place upstairs, somewhere, without him. On his cellphone, he called the auction house, whose receptionist told him that he had walked one block in the wrong direction and offered to send a car to retrieve him. He declined and hung up. "We won't make that mistake again," he said to me.

The correct address turned out to be a single-story warehouse directly behind us. Having traveled here thinking I'd bear witness to the last gasps of a dying institution, I was stunned to see how modern the fur business had become. The facilities were clean, contemporary, and well lighted, with waiting rooms furnished by plush new couches that did not smell of cigarettes or alcohol or fur, and a fully stocked cafeteria and dining room. Through a glass window, you could see the auction itself—dozens of traders seated at individual desks, their cellphones flipped open and their laptop computers powered up as they communicated in real time with buyers from England, Greece, Russia, China, and South Korea, attention fixed on an auctioneer who stood at the front of the room, announcing each lot in a voice so methodical and mellifluous you'd think he was calling a square dance:

> For-tee-three in the front—yes lot one-fif-tee-a-one—be-fore you
>   turn-a the page
> I'm now bid for-tee-four—in the center, for-tee-four
> For-tee-five is bid—now six in the center
> Seven in the center? No? Ho! Ho! Ho!

When that man banged his gavel, people in the room applauded.

Beyond this room, my father ushered me through a back door and into the fur business that I knew best: hardy, gray-haired men with eyeglasses dangling precipitously from their ears, who had finished the day's work and had gathered around tables to drink beer, play poker, paw at half-eaten deli sandwiches, and smoke musty brown Dutch Masters Presidentes. When they went home for the night, they'd be dressed immaculately in button-down shirts, pleated slacks, and loafers, but for now they were camouflaged by long white work coats, spackled in occasional droplets of the same musky concoction that repeated washings could never completely extract from my father's clothes.

Then there was the fur itself, lurking in the deepest reaches of the warehouse, a fluorescent cavern where the air was kept cold and thin by refrigeration units. While they waited to be sold, the skins sat piled up on pallets, stripped from the bodies of wild animals and pounded flat, staring with uniform vacancy through emptied-out eye sockets: snow-white lynx cats, chestnut-brown sable, sleek gray sable, coyotes and ermines, wolverines and squirrels, and beavers whose round pelts had been smashed into circular shapes as if they were giant pancakes. The mere sight of these mute artifacts—just the feeling of my sneakers slipping slightly on the concrete floor from the oils—was enough to transport me back to my father's old, vacated offices on West Twenty-ninth Street.

There were certain former confederates whom my father hoped he would not encounter: "This weasel," he said to me, pointing not to an animal but to a man, a wayward former customer who had ordered 150 pieces of dressed raccoon fur and then returned the entire shipment, claiming that what he really wanted were badgers. "He's embarrassed to say hello to me. Such a schmuck." And still others wouldn't be attending the sale at all, like David Karsch, a seventy-four-year-old former fur broker from Alaska who, days earlier, had pleaded guilty to federal charges of conspiracy to restrain trade, over an alleged attempt to rig the price of otter pelts.

Those fellow furriers whom my father did want to see consistently reacted to his appearance with an emotion I had no idea he was capable of eliciting: awe. Some of them wanted to know why he'd been absent from the auction for so many years; others seemed nervous that he'd come back with the specific intention of outbidding them on whatever skins they were planning to buy; and some appeared to be under the mistaken impression that he was dead. "I knew I'd see you sooner or later," one rival told him with feigned relief, "because only the good die young."

"You know people in this business," my father replied. "They only stop when they hit a brick wall."

The drug stories began to flow as freely as the auctioneer's incantations. From my father's lips, I heard tales of Baruch Steinschneider, an Orthodox Jew who liked to fire guns and drive four-by-four trucks and who could be seen the morning after an all-night binge "eyes red, gritting his teeth with a yarmulke on his head"; and Noel Heller, a furrier who liked to deal a little coke on the side and became a coke dealer who liked to sell a little fur on the side, who died in prison of a heart attack after conviction for possession and trafficking.

Other longtime peers in attendance shared their recollections. Mason Haynes, a sturdy, bearded fur trader from Michigan, a latter-day Paul Bunyan, who'd come to pass along a tall but true tale of his own: "I came by your store," he told my father, as if reminiscing about some old fraternity prank, "the door was open, and there you were on the floor. I didn't know if you were dead!" He punctuated the observation with a laugh.

My father chuckled, too. "I was just takin' a nap," he said.

Even the business adversaries who obviously hated my father's guts had fond drug-related memories. Helmut Lebensalter was a husky, well-dressed gentleman with the carefully groomed facial hair and unplaceable European accent of a James Bond villain. He was looking over some skins at one of the inspection tables in the back of the auction house when he saw my father coming; he greeted him by asking, "Are you still manipulating the markets, Gerry?"

This initiated a long lecture from my father about the best point in a fiscal cycle to buy fur ("when nobody else wants it"), and why one should never invest in the market with borrowed money, and a reiteration of his philosophy that he would never leave the fur business alive. (I believe his exact words were "You must die—they must kill you. If you hear that I'm retiring, I must be sick.")

"Did you hear the professor?" Helmut asked me, not really expecting an answer.

As my father walked away to say hello to another old client, Helmut turned to me and said quietly, "Ask him about the Egyptian Garden." I thought for certain he'd slipped me a coded message—a fragmentary allusion to some foreign trip they'd once taken or an outrageously lucrative deal they'd pulled off, but it turned out to be the name of a bar where they used to get high together.

Another colleague, Brad Resnick, who rented a portion of my father's upstairs office for some fifteen years, summarized for me how my father had been able to dominate his competitors. "They hated to come to him," he said. "He's the hardest person that God ever created. He's an extremist, but he's right."

The environment of the auction helped my father remember the excitement and adrenaline of the fur business, but it also seemed to trick him into thinking he was still participating in it at full throttle. When he wasn't avidly drinking soda, he was restlessly chewing gum, and when a conversation became especially heated, he would sometimes preserve his gum on the lid of his soda can, leaving the half-chewed wad on display until he had finished his discourse and was ready to start chewing it again. He would drift to distant ends of the auction house, become involved in exchanges that went on for a half hour or an hour at a time, and then wander back to me as if in a daze, with no realization of how much time had elapsed.

So I left my father at the auction house, walked back to our hotel room, determined which Canadian television stations broadcast *The Simpsons* and *South Park* and at what times of day, and spent the rest of the afternoon transcribing an interview for a magazine article I was working on.

I slept poorly that night and woke up early the next morning with a cold, probably the result of my prolonged exposure to cigarette smoke and unknown elements in the uncontaminated Canadian atmosphere that were toxic only to the central nervous system of New Yorkers. My father was already up, unaware that I was awake; I could hear him preparing for a swim in the hotel pool. He was breathing slowly and deeply as he changed into a pair of trunks and a hotel-issue bathing robe. With each exhalation, he seemed to be urging himself to continue forward and face the day.

"How am I gonna do this?"

Breath.

"But I gotta do this."

Breath.

"I can't do this."

Breath.

"But I gotta do this."

Breath.

I was still in a state of partial wakefulness, so I can't be sure if I heard his words correctly. But I'm fairly certain I didn't dream them.

For weeks it felt as if we were making no progress. Our telephone conversations had become less frequent and more cursory, usually about his health or his business or the weather he was getting upstate, and when I would remind him about our designs to travel widely and reach deep into his past, his response was always non-committal. "I know, I know," he would say.

Then, abruptly, he became passionately, vehemently insistent that we follow through on our plans. He had become fixated on a scene in a book I wrote that was set at a friend's wedding, where I tried Ecstasy for the first time. In the rush of blood, endorphins, and enhanced feelings brought on by the drug, I confessed that one of my first impulses—after my overwhelming urges to go to the bathroom and lay every woman at the wedding banquet—was to call my parents and encourage them to take the drug with me. What stopped me was the realization, even in my agitated, over-sensitive state, that these were precisely the kinds of phone calls that my father used to make when he got high.

I was sitting alone in a hotel room in Memphis, working on a story and tinkering with a complicated cellphone I had recently bought, when my father called to tell me what he interpreted these passages to mean. The LCD display of my phone had gone blank, and as I stared at my own reflection in its darkened glass screen, I heard on its speakerphone my father's digitized voice say, "When you're high, it brings out the true part of you. The *best* part of you.

"I'm a work in progress, David," he said. "I'm still not a thousand percent comfortable with myself—if I were, would I be talking like this? I always wanted to be the person I felt I was when I was high." He sounded so certain that I was in agreement with him that I didn't have the nerve to tell him he had misconstrued my point entirely.

A few days later, we were making our arrangements for a week-long trip to New Orleans. At my father's insistence, we purchased our plane tickets in advance but reserved no hotel rooms nor rental cars: these remaining essentials, he said, would be taken care of when we arrived and no sooner, and then only on a day-by-day, as-needed basis. It was a most un-Dad-like way to travel, and yet it bore all the unmistakable attributes of a Gerry Itzkoff production: carefree and spontaneous, disorganized, impulsive and unnecessarily risky, demanding total freedom and utterly ignorant of consequences. Which were the expressions of the true part of him?

At the start of May, we touched down in Louisiana with no compass, no street maps and no GPS, no itinerary, and no sense of where we would be sleeping that night. (Had we been the least bit conscientious about planning the trip, we probably would not have arrived in the middle of the New Orleans Jazz Fest.) In a rental car we hired at the airport that morning, I was driving my father along the same routes he once traveled with his father in vehicles laden with mink or muskrat skins so valuable and vital to their business they would drive them to the airport and load them onto planes themselves, as if transporting elderly, infirm family members or irreplaceable works of art.

My father thought he would be able to recognize these thoroughly traveled streets on sight, but they were unfamiliar to him now; the sea-level strips of pavement buffered on either side by untamed and unending swampland had long ago been supplanted by elevated highways that bypassed the bayous entirely. Not quite two years had passed since Hurricane Katrina tore through the area, and a protracted recovery process, only recently initiated, had done little to mask the scars of the devastation. Even the most heavily trafficked avenues were still cracked and caked with a thin, permanent layer of red clay, as if the storm had dispersed only a few weeks ago, and any street sign with more than ten or eleven letters—not uncommon in a town whose every alleyway and cul-de-sac is named for an American revolutionary or a French monument—had been bent beyond readability by heavy winds. The damage was so rampant that after a few hours of driving, it became dull to point it out. My father was irritated that the population dispersion he had been promised by the news media did not make rush-hour traffic any less congested, and he was fearful that after he'd been away from the city for so long, none of its remaining residents would recognize him.

The circumstances of our last visits to New Orleans could not have been more different. Seven years ago, I had traveled to the French Quarter for a raucous bachelor party during which I was never far from a bar or a strip club. For my father, this was the city where he had at least twice attempted to attend college and at least twice dropped out, where he had learned the family business from his father, who spent six months out of every year apart from his wife and his children entrenched in the Hotel Monteleone, doing battle with the hundreds of other furriers who were once as plentiful to the Gulf Coast as piping plovers and whooping cranes, and sending home autocratic letters every day to his hapless dropout son. My father had spent nearly half of his own life here, and yet he had not been back in nearly twenty years, not since he came to sit at his father's hospital bed, watch him slip into a coma, and never regain consciousness. After this visit, it was hard to say when he might be back.

We were driving over the Lake Pontchartrain Causeway, a narrow twenty-four-mile-long suspension bridge that sits obliviously atop six hundred square miles of restless and capricious water. As I watched for any rain that would fall and compel the lake to swallow us up, my father began to tell me about something that had happened to him a few weeks ago in the Catskills.

He had been swimming at the gym and was toweling off in the locker room when an Orthodox Jew at a nearby bench took notice of him and approached him.

"Are you Jewish?" the man asked my father.

Despite the invitation to trouble that such a question usually portends, my father nonetheless answered it honestly and in the affirmative.

"Were you circumcised?" the stranger asked him. Again without stopping to contemplate the motives behind the line of questioning, my father answered yes.

"Really?" the man responded. "Because to me it looks like they didn't finish the job." Then he added: "Do you mind if I check for myself?"

The imaginary version of my father I held in my mind's eye absolutely floored me by consenting to the man's request. The Jew beheld my father's naked body and inspected his penis manually and concluded that his initial observation was correct: there was still a small amount of foreskin remaining.

"No," he said. "The circumcision was not done correctly. It was not completed." He suggested to my father that the problem be rectified as quickly as possible, and my father, in a voice no doubt as calm and composed as the one in which he related the story to me, declined, and the conversation was ended.

"Now," my father said, turning to his only son, whom he loved, "why do you think this man did that?"

I could think of many reasons why an unfamiliar man might lurk in a locker room with intentions of placing his hands on my father's manhood, most of them stemming from nasty, apocryphal rumors about the sexual habits of Orthodox Jews that got spread around the secular summer camps I attended. But when I explained this to my father—that just because a man grows a long beard and wears tefillin and asks to touch your penis, it does not necessarily make him a person of faith—he disagreed.

"David, don't you understand that the Jewish faith teaches that you cannot get into heaven unless you've been circumcised?" His voice cracked, and his eyes welled with tears of pride. "He wasn't doing it for himself, he was doing it for me. It was a mitzvah."

As with any story in my father's possession, it turned out that this was not the first time he had told it, or the fifth, or even the twenty-fifth. He had already recounted it to just about every friend and colleague he could get on the phone, mostly men his own age, and so far every single one had sided with his interpretation of the story (or so they told him, or so he told me). It was difficult enough for me to listen to on its merits: among its details about penises, and my father's penis, and observant Jews, and observant Jews touching my father's penis, there was nothing that I ever wanted to hear about again. It reminded me that there was a gap between me and my father wider than Lake Pontchartrain and at the same time no wider than my father's last remaining piece of foreskin.

We spent the night in a motel room on the outskirts of Orleans Parish, next door to a Denny's that was fully stocked and furnished but had not been open in months because it could not hire enough employees to keep itself in business. Our accommodations weren't particularly inviting, either. "Well, we didn't get killed last night," my father declared as we checked out. "I thought we'd get butt-fucked for sure."

That morning marked my first visit to the campus of Tulane University and my father's first in over fifty years. The residential areas seemed no worse for Katrina's onslaught; the dormitories were weather-beaten, though my father assured me they looked no different in his day, and beaded necklaces and Mardi Gras masks hung harmoniously from trees, but maybe they had always been there, too. In ninety-degree weather, the students strode the grounds in shorts and T-shirts bearing proud slogans like I STILL GO TO TULANE and GO FEMA YOURSELF. With its Gothic quad-rangles unabashedly modeled on Princeton's, unabashedly pla-giarized from Oxford and Cambridge, Tulane was stirring in me a pleasant sensation I rarely felt about my college experience; I be-lieve it's called nostalgia.

The same could not be said of my father, who became more deeply lost in his memories, the farther we trod. To him, the campus was a pastoral 110-acre reminder of days consumed by classes, studies, and ze fukshuns of Dr. Goto, a high-stakes card game called Bourré, and evenings spent riding the bus to my grandfather's fur business in the French Quarter, working with the greasy, musky skins until midnight or one in the morning, riding the St. Charles streetcar as near as it would bring him to campus, then walking the remaining miles back to his room.

My grandfather paid him erratically for his obligatory services; on occasional weeks he gave him fifty dollars and most weeks nothing at all. My father had no dress clothes—"Not a fucking sport jacket from Alexander's," he said—and no car to drive on the weekends, when most students abandoned the campus and left him in solitude. Though he never achieved the rank of sopho-more, my father said he had learned a valuable lesson at Tulane: "You can't have too much money, and you can never be too much in control of your own life. You can never trust anybody."

He took out his cellphone and wandered off to call my mother, to repeat to her how he was made to work long hours at my grand-father's shop and never had a car or any spending money. I stood where I was and called Amy to tell her that in the days leading up to this trip, I had convinced myself I was doing a good deed for my father, giving him the emotional support for a journey he never would have taken on his own, but now I realized I'd made a mistake, that this whole thing was an act of cruelty. When my father returned, he ran out the afternoon pointing angrily at the bookstores and student centers the university had lacked in his day, then stretched himself beneath one of the ancient oak trees on the main quad that refused to be moved by time and tide. I hadn't seen him look so worn down in a while.

We returned to the city via St. Charles Avenue in search of a hotel in the French Quarter, with my father playing the role of navigator and myself in the pilot's seat. I found it hard not to lose my temper when a traffic light would turn green and he seemed not to know which way to go, or when his lack of guidance nearly steered us off the end of Canal Street and into the mighty Mississippi. It was no different, I figured, than when my father was driving and he would routinely snap at me or my mother or whoever was seated in the passenger seat when he was in desperate need of directions or stuck in traffic behind a grimy station wagon teeming with Hassidim. He left me in the car for some length of time while he cased a waterside Hilton hotel, only to emerge and declare that he didn't feel like staying there. Next he had me drop him off at the Hotel Monteleone, which had served as my grandfather's de facto residence and whose letterhead decorated almost all his correspondence during his time in Louisiana. It did not take my father long to step in, step out, and conclude that this was not where we would be spending the night.

The only tangible possession I have to remember my grandfather by is a postcard he sent me in 1988, when I was twelve years old, a few months before he died. On its front is a photograph of a young woman in a bikini, kneeling provocatively on a sandy beach as an alligator approaches her from behind, its jaws widening in preparation to bite her on the ass. Beneath the picture is a caption that reads, "WOW! We alligators sure have fun in Louisiana." On the back of the postcard, my grandfather inscribed the following message:

Dear David,
    A few months back I promised to write you, So—"HERE GOES!"

As Ever,
Bob

P.S. I'm going in to the Alligator Business!

I cannot recall my grandfather making that specific promise to me, but this single piece of correspondence says a lot about how I remember him. He was a randy, lively person, among the few offspring of Russian Jewish immigrants to have picked up a conversant vocabulary of Cajun curse words and Creole slang, the sort of man who wouldn't allow the rest of his family to order dinner at a restaurant table until he'd had a chocolate milk shake first, and who got his laughs by inviting his young grandson into his study, sitting him on his lap, and confessing that he was the man who had assassinated John F. Kennedy.

In fact, during his lifetime, my grandfather was a persistent and diligent letter writer, and my father has saved hundreds of pages of the mail he wrote on a daily basis. Among the communiqués that my father holds most dearly, if not quite fondly, is a set of letters my grandfather wrote to him in 1964, a few years after they became business partners, which circumscribe an incident now known as the Primeaux Affair.

Belus Primeaux was a West Louisiana furrier who had written to Bob and Gerald Itzkoff about some goods he wanted to sell them, right around the time that my grandfather was headed south to Louisiana for the winter. When my father attempted to convey this offer to my grandfather, my grandfather mistakenly concluded that my father was somehow withholding other crucial information. The misunderstanding inspired my grandfather to compose this first letter, dated simply "Wednesday, 1964," in the same elegant cursive that graces the back of my alligator postcard:

Dear Gerald,

In view of the fact that I was not informed as to the contents of Primeaux's letter and having not received the original letter sent to "me," I think you ought to have your "Head" examined! This . . . is a very serious matter with me. I could itemize quite a list of objections I have to your conduct, in fact a very long list!

Let it be understood that the following is in order:

I want a letter written each and every day!

You make no appointments for Monday nights that may interfere with you taking your mother to her Mah Jong [sic] game.

You give your mother $50—each week.

In the future, you are forbidden to super-impose your judgement for my experienced opinion or desires, as for instance the phone answering service.

~~This~~ As I said before, There is a long list of objections & the Primeaux affair is minor but important in principle—Of

greater importance would be your failure to remember a
Wedding anniversary or a Birthday or Anything!

As Ever,
Bob

History has lost my father's reply, but its contents can be reasonably deduced from the relevant portions of the next letter that
my grandfather sent him, dated November 16, 1964:

Dear Gerald,
    In answer to your letter of the 13th:
    #1 I make no apologies for what I wrote!
    #2 If I wanted to fulminate our partnership, "I'd do it!"
    #3 If you can't stand the treatment or consideration you are
getting from me then you do it "Quit!"
    . . .
    In the meantime you are still in possession of information
which belongs to me, I demand this information immediately! This is the sum total of my demands and which you interpret as "<u>Insults!</u>"

I remain
YOUR FUCKIN FATHER.

P.S. I still don't have Primeaux's letter. What do I have to do to
get it?

Again, my father's reply is absent from the sequence of exchanges. When my father writes to me now, usually in the form of
a short email, I let the note sit in my inbox for a few days before I

reply to it, if I do at all. No such luxuries were afforded to him when he communicated with his father; prompt responses were demanded and extracted from him by force if necessary. Every letter they traded was a wide-open venue to air any grievance, no matter how consequential or petty, to be discussed in the language that came most naturally to them, before the sieve of rational thought could filter out their impulsive emotions.

From the perspective of anyone other than my father, it is possible to read those letters and be both astounded and amused by them; even within our extended family, the Primeaux Affair has become a kind of inside joke, an affectionate snapshot of my grandfather at his most intractable and idiosyncratic. But to the man to whom the letters were addressed, it is impossible to contemplate them and not be seized by an intensely personal and incommunicable pain, not be transported back to a time when he was a son and not a father and could not make his intentions known to the one man he wanted more than any other in the world to understand him.

What I got from my grandfather was a bawdy postcard; what my father got from him was a philosophy of life. He was taught to be disciplined, to hold values and have convictions—to have convictions *in* conviction, to know that there were times when a man must hold on to what he believes even when no one else around him will believe him. He learned that there is a man called Father whose job it is to tell you things, especially when you don't want to believe them, and when this man called Father tells you something, it can be counted upon and it must be believed, because the opposite condition—not believing in Father—means not having certainty, and that is a circumstance too horrible and terrifying to contemplate.

After surveying the hotels of the French Quarter, my father and

I settled in—by chance, at the same hotel where I had stayed during that bachelor party and done terrible things over the side of its Bourbon Street balconies. When we checked in, my father made a beeline for the bathroom. He seemed to think its tiled walls and not-quite-airtight door offered him some degree of soundproofing as he engaged in a heated cellphone conversation with someone I quickly deduced was my mother. Though I could not hear everything he said, a sufficient measure of his unrestrained invective escaped into the bedroom for me to figure out the subject of his tirade.

". . . I am *not* doing this with him again, Maddy! Never in a hundred million years! . . ."

". . . He is *ungrateful*. He is wild and he is unrestrained. You can't control him! . . ."

". . . but he doesn't talk like that when he's on the phone to his girlfriend! . . ."

". . . so then tell me what the hell is his problem with *me*?"

With nowhere else to go, and nowhere to sit or stand in the room where I could not hear him, I let these rough fragments scour over me in wave after abrasive wave. I would have preferred for my father's fierce critique to have continued indefinitely than to have felt my heart seize up at the moment when his conversation ended and the room fell silent. Soon I would have to look him in the eyes again, and he would read from my defeated face that I had overheard the most crucial portions of a confession he had never meant for me to hear, thus gaining knowledge of feelings I was never meant to know he possessed. And then, somehow, we would have to get past even this.

HOW WE ARGUE IN MY FAMILY

I. Opening Statements

"You know that I could hear you in there, right? I mean, I could hear every word that you said. Is this what you think of me? Is this how you talk about me when I'm not around, when you think I'm not listening?"

"Now, David, let's just take it easy, okay?"

"No, Dad, I don't want to take it easy. We're going to talk about this now."

"All right. But I don't think you're going to like some of the things I have to say."

II. The Recitation of Grievances

"I feel that you've been very disrespectful to me at times on this trip. You've been very short with me when we're driving in the car. You snap at me when I don't know the directions, when I don't know which way to turn."

II.a. So?

"So?"

"So I haven't lived here for almost fifty years. And I see the faces that you make when I'm talking to other people. You look like you could die. What, are you embarrassed of me?"

III. The Escalation of Force

"Because half the time you don't know these people. And you talk to everybody you encounter like they're your best friends. Why do you find it so easy to open up to people you've never met before, but getting you to talk to me is like pulling teeth?"

"I don't know, David. I guess that's
just my way. What does it matter to
you, anyway?"

IV. The Queen's Gambit

"You go around acting like you can
behave any way you want. Don't you
realize that you're alienating the
people who are closest to you? I think
you're going to look up one day and
realize that you're all alone."

"Who? Who am I alienating?"

"Me. My sister."

IV.a. The Queen's Gambit Accepted

"Oh, is that so? You think you know
what your sister thinks?"

"We've talked about you. I think she
would agree with me."

"You sure about that? You want me to
call her on the phone right now and
ask her?"

"N-no."

V. The Invocation of the Immutable Past

"You have always been a willful person, David. Even from the time you were a little boy, when we would go for drives in the car, do you know that you used to reach up from the backseat and change the radio stations I was listening to?"

"What the fuck does that have to do with anything? You listen to me, you monster, you have no right to invoke my childhood. You missed half of it because you were constantly high on drugs. You have no idea who I was then, and you have no idea who I am now."

"David, I can't keep apologizing to you for all the years that I was on drugs. I'm not taking them now, am I? I'm not high now, am I?"

VI. Outright Revisionism

"Do you know that in all the time I used to get high, I never once raised my hand to you or your sister? I never once got physical with either of you. You know that, don't you?"

"Oh my God, that is so not true! You
say this all the time, and I always correct you, and you never remember.
You think that if you say it enough
times, that makes it true."

VII. Turnover on Downs

"I think you still have a lot of issues to
deal with from my drug use."

"And your problem is that you're incapable of seeing people as anything
other than who they used to be."

VIII. The Threat to Throw the Chair out the
Window

"I think I'm going to throw this
goddamn chair out the goddamn
window."

"Don't do that."

IX. Closing Statements with Partial Apology

"Look, David, I apologize that you
overheard me talking to your mother
before. I feel terrible about that. It's
like I keep telling you: I'm a work in
progress, okay? I'm not going to get

everything right all the time. Now do
you forgive me?"

"Okay. Fine."

X. The Changing of the Subject

"I'm starving. You want to go downstairs and get something to eat?"

"Sure."

CHAPTER 9

On the morning of our third day in New Orleans, my father awoke reinvigorated. Prior to our trip, his greatest concern had been that everyone he once knew in the city would be gone, and those who remained would no longer remember him or choose to acknowledge him. Following our fight and reconciliatory oyster dinner, the pendulum of his emotions was free to swing in the opposite direction. Daylight had barely broken, and he was already dialing away at his cellphone, calling information in search of phone numbers: for a woman with whom he used to play cards at Tulane, who he had heard was unmarried and still living in Louisiana; for a former roommate who had fled all the way to Arizona to escape his gambling debts; and for another roommate who had apparently made a fortune as an executive for a Texas-based cafeteria-services corporation. It did not matter if these people lived in time zones where the sun had not yet risen, or if his son, in the bed right next to his, was not yet ready to accept the fact that it was morning. He wanted to get someone, anyone, on the phone, and he wanted to talk right away.

He was especially concerned about a woman named Adelphia, a New Orleans native who was about his age and who had started working for my grandfather at around the same time he did. I did not have to ask if my grandfather paid her the same wages that my father received, or if her duties were commensurate with his; she was a woman, and she was black. But she remained with my grandfather for the duration of his Louisiana career, and she was at his hospital bedside every day as he suffered the progressively worsening stages of a subdural hematoma, and she was with him on the day he died. Despite the crucial supporting role she played in my family's history, I had never met Adelphia, although I had once briefly encountered her daughter, Esther, who worked in the hospitality department of the hotel where my friends and I stayed during our bachelor-party debauchery. She sent a complimentary fruit basket to our room before we proceeded to throw up all over our accommodations.

It seemed certain that Adelphia and her family would have been displaced by Hurricane Katrina, and we had no idea when or if they might have returned to New Orleans. Months before our trip, when I first sat down with my father to review his life history, he had asked me to help him use various search engines and other computer tools to see if we could find Adelphia's telephone number or home address. But for as much as my father professed to care about her, he could not remember what last name she went by, and all the phone numbers we found that might have been hers simply rang without end.

This morning, with the help of a Louisiana phone book and a directory assistance website, my father had managed to call just about every number that might have been Adelphia's, politely disposing of the respondents who turned out not to be her, and diligently making note of each listing that went unanswered. Somewhat deflated, he snapped his phone shut and went into the bathroom to take a shower. And then Adelphia called back.

I answered my father's phone, and in a soft Southern twang, she explained to me that she had spent the morning locked out on her porch. Though she had no answering machine, she had noticed my father's name on her caller ID when she at last got back into her house. She said that we could come by to visit as soon as we wanted; knowing my father, I told her that would most likely be right away. I did not interrupt my father's shower to tell him that Adelphia had been located, or that she had located herself; I waited until he emerged from the bathroom, with a towel around his waist and an electric toothbrush whirring in his mouth, at which point he started to cry. The tears streaming down his cheeks began to commingle with the toothpaste froth that had accumulated around his lips, and he looked positively elated.

Adelphia's home in the Garden District was only a few miles from our hotel, and the directions she gave us were precise, yet we managed to drive past it at least once or twice before we arrived. It was our first visit to a predominantly black neighborhood in the city, and our first opportunity to view up close how arbitrary Katrina's devastation had been. No structure had completely escaped the hurricane's punishing touch, but on any given block, the damage from house to house could run a frustrating, heartbreaking gamut; one building might be missing substantial parts of its roof or its walls, or leveled to its foundation, while its immediate neighbor sustained nothing more permanent than superficial water damage.

Adelphia was waiting for us on the lawn in front of her townhouse, but my father did not recognize her right away. A small, compact woman of sixty-six, she was now dyeing her short hair a bright copper red, and her expressive eyes were hidden behind a pair of glasses that my father had never seen her wear. With a combined 133 years of life between them, they hugged each other, and my father began to cry again. She was a patient woman with a perpetual, genuine smile, but the smile, too, was a disguise; it concealed a wellspring of endurance whose depths had been plumbed by repeated misfortune and tragedy and whose bottom had yet to be found.

She was no older than sixteen or seventeen when she began working for my grandfather, a man she referred to even in the present day as "Mister Bob," and her memories of him were fairly consistent with my father's: "Mister Bob, he hollered at me, too," Adelphia explained. "People used to say, 'Why do you work for that Jew? He always hollerin' at you.' I say, 'Ah, he don't mean half of what he say.'" She would have known about his temperament from her first husband, Ray, who was already in my grandfather's employ when Adelphia joined the business; Ray was an inveterate drunk who rarely showed up sober for work, if at all, but she forgave him, perhaps because she had her own habit of betting her wages on horse races.

Adelphia and Ray eventually split up, but not before they produced two sons, Patrick and Tracy. Tracy had been a heroin addict for most of his life and had done time in the Angola penitentiary for felony drug possession, but Adelphia still referred to him as her "best child," as in "I tell everybody my best child went to prison." He had been spared incarceration once before, when he was caught stealing money he was supposed to deposit in my grandfather's bank account; my grandfather appeared at the trial to testify on Tracy's behalf. (According to my father, my grandfather told the court, "The bank put money in the hands of a drug

addict. What do you want him to do?") When Tracy was jailed for
a later offense, he got seven years shaved off his sentence for defending a female guard from the attacks of a far more dangerous
male inmate.

For ten years, Adelphia worked as a New Orleans cabdriver
even as she continued to work for my grandfather, and after he
died, she took a job as a cook and housekeeper for a fraternity
house at Tulane, whose brothers were so enamored of her that
they paid for her to travel with them on their annual spring-break
visits to Florida. When Katrina came to town, Adelphia and her
second husband, a man whose round, ebullient face gazed upon
us from photographs that hung throughout the house, wasted no
time in evacuating the city, driving first to Baton Rouge and then
to Greenwood, Mississippi. For many months after the waters
had receded, they resisted going home, anticipating the cataclysm that would be waiting for them, and her husband, who had
prostate cancer, never made the trip. "He passed," Adelphia explained.

She returned to New Orleans to find the roof of her house
missing and its insides largely flooded. The first contractor she
paid to repair the damage simply absconded with her money. So
she called on Patrick and Tracy, who helped her rebuild the
house. Now she lived there with Esther—who did not remember
our earlier encounter at the hotel, the fruit basket, or the vomit—
and Esther's daughters, a trio of school-age girls who dressed
in kneesocks and respectfully referred to Adelphia as "Grandmother."

I should confess here that I am not telling this story in the
order it was presented to me. Adelphia did not convey the complete details of her life and her whereabouts since Katrina to my
father and me in a single uninterrupted telling; I had to assemble

it from the fragments she was able to dole out in the brief inter-
vals between the lengthy soliloquies that my father had come to
perform for her. We had barely settled into Adelphia's living room,
with its new carpeting and vinyl couches assembled around a big-
screen television enshrined in a wobbly plastic wall unit, when my
father began to recount the story of how my grandfather split
up the family business in hopes that it would compel my father to
give up his drug habit—a story that Adelphia knew well, because
she had consulted with my grandfather on his decision.

"Do you know, Adelphia, how much that man sacrificed for
me?" my father asked rhetorically, his voice breaking, his eyes
once again welling with tears, and his face in frighteningly close
proximity to hers. "There is no one—*no one*—who helped me more
than my father. He's the only one who finally helped me get clean."

Everything he had said up to this point I could dismiss as the
harmless rationalizations of an old man, but this last statement
struck me as patently untrue. It ignored the honor roll of pleading
friends who had, over the years, begged him to seek help for his
problem; the cooperation of other family members who had
stood by him through other, more traditional treatments that did
not work; and the immeasurable support of my mother, who
could have simply walked away after any number of failed thera-
pies, abortive institutionalizations, and foreseeable relapses, but
never did. I said nothing, and the performance continued on.

As we followed Adelphia upstairs to the second story of her
home, where she sat herself down in front of a smaller television
set, at a coffee table strewn with blank lottery tickets, Social Security checks, and uncompleted government forms, my father
began the next segment of his oration. This time he told her the
story about rummaging around in the glove compartment of the
family sedan and discovering my grandfather's glass eye.

It was not until this particular recitation of the story that I learned my father waited to confront my grandfather about this until they had been business partners for many years.

The only reason he was able to open up to my grandfather so courageously and so completely is because my father was high on cocaine at the time.

Now, here's the punch line: having related this tale to Adelphia, my father asked her, "Was it better that I could only tell my father how I felt about him when I was high, or would it have been better if I never told him at all?"

It was a neat bit of sleight of hand that my father had pulled off, one that his conscious mind might not even have been aware of. This was the sort of loaded, binary question a pollster asks when he already knows the results he wants to produce; and it lacked an obvious third choice: find the strength to tell your father how you feel without having to get high at all. But given the two choices offered to her, Adelphia came back surprisingly quickly with the answer I'm certain my father wanted to hear all along: "I think it's better that he knew how you felt about him before he died," she said.

Adelphia knew my father's history maybe better than I did; she had seen it firsthand. In the years since they last saw each other, it was her life that had become a complete mystery, not his. But she was too tolerant of life's torments to ever ask him to yield the floor, and he was too caught up in his self-perpetuating narrative to stop. He was going to keep reciting his mortal offenses to her until she told him that the life he had lived was its own act of contrition and that no further penance was required. And still I said nothing.

On Adelphia's television, the courtroom reality show she had been watching was interrupted by a news bulletin announcing that a tornado watch was in effect for New Orleans and the surrounding area. Within minutes the report was made redundant as the skies turned gray and let loose with a thick, persistent rain; one moment the street outside Adelphia's house was dry and cracked and begging like a transient for sustenance—the next, it was so deeply flooded that cars could no longer drive, and pedestrians were attempting to ford it with gardening tools. In another hour or so, a television anchor announced that it was the most rain the city had seen since Hurricane Katrina—only five or six inches but enough to send me running to the windows every few minutes in attempts to convince myself that what I was seeing was actually happening. There was something pitiless about it, that anyone who had been made to bear these conditions once before should have to experience them again so soon.

Adelphia never stirred from her seat, not even when Esther came into the room to declare, "If it really keeps raining, we're getting out of here, sister!" Nor was my father the least bit dissuaded in the slow and ceaseless recitation of his ongoing harangue. He told Adelphia he was unimpressed with the quality of leadership in the African-American community and that those who stayed behind in New Orleans when Katrina touched down and attempted to ride out the storm got what they deserved; they had no reasonable expectation for the government to provide for them in the aftermath, he felt. "If FEMA tried to give *me* a trailer," he said, "I wouldn't take it. I'd rather sleep on the floor." Adelphia nodded in agreement, as she had through the previous portions of the sermon.

On a break from talking about himself, my father began to tell Adelphia about me and the passage from my first book that he had been fixated on lately. He wanted to lecture her about the scene where I described my experience taking Ecstasy and his misbegotten interpretation of that moment. Though I had already com-

mitted that incident to paper for anyone to read, I found it uncomfortable to hear my father describe my past drug use, in my
presence, to a sixty-six-year-old woman whom I'd known only
for a couple of hours, and who, for all her worldly experience,
probably had no idea what Ecstasy was.

So I asked him to stop. "Dad," I said, "can we please not talk
about this right now?"

"Why?" he said. "Why not?"

"Because I don't want you to," I said. "Isn't that enough?"

Genuinely confused, he answered, "But you're not my father."

That was all I needed to hear. There had never been anyone
who could tell him what to do or not to do, or convince him of
anything he did not already believe, except his father, and that
man had been dead since 1989. I excused myself from the room,
went downstairs, and walked out the front door of Adelphia's
house. Before the storm, I had the good fortune to park our rental
car on a hill next door, in front of a tenement house wallpapered
in bumper stickers calling for the reelection of Representative
William Jefferson, the nine-term Louisiana congressman who
would be indicted on corruption and bribery charges the following month. I unlocked the car and sat inside, listened to the radio,
and watched the rain subside and the flood recede.

Later, my father came out of the house with Adelphia behind
him. They hugged and kissed each other farewell, and I stepped
out of the car to tell her goodbye. "David," she said gently, "be
good to your father. Listen to what he says. He needs you." I told
her only that I would try. When my father asked me for the car
keys so that this time he could drive, I allowed it.

At our fourth hotel of the week, while my father fell asleep to a
late-night television broadcast of *Red River,* I sneaked out of our
room to be comforted by the recurrent hum of the nearest

soda machine. Illuminated by its glow, I called Amy to tell her of recent events—the visit to Adelphia's house, the rains, the constant fighting.

"You don't sound so good," she said.

"This hasn't gone at all like I thought it would," I said. "When we get back to New York, I am coming straight home to you and I am never leaving. I don't want my life to turn out like this."

"It doesn't have to," she said.

My father and I woke up on our last full day in New Orleans, transformed into a pair of grifters with no obligations or commitments, no permanent address, no possessions, and no imperative to do anything except whatever was necessary to sustain us until the next day. I was exhausted, but my father was becoming more energetic and manic by the minute, and when it came time for us to finally leave Louisiana, I wasn't sure I'd be able to convince him to get on the plane.

Today we had nothing but time on our hands, so my father took us out to Raceland, a rural community about forty miles southwest of New Orleans, serviced by two local highways and perhaps a single traffic light where they intersected. He had brought us here looking for a family named the Fonsecas, a clan of fur traders he and my grandfather had done business with for generations. He seemed to think that if we simply cruised up and down the streets of Raceland long enough, he would eventually recognize their ancestral home on sight. Raceland is a small town but not that small, and after several passes back and forth on Highway 1, we could not find the house, nor anyone who seemed to know where they might live, except a pair of drunks in a run-down gas station who gave us completely contradictory directions. "If we could just find a sheriff's station," my father kept repeating.

Abandoning any pretense of effort or challenge, I pulled out my phone, typed the name Fonseca into a search engine, and came up with their address instantly. We turned a single corner and there was their house, more or less exactly as my father remembered it. "I should have known," he said, resentful that he had been unable to recall a single obscure detail from a life he led over twenty years ago.

In his heyday, my grandfather had done business primarily with the Fonseca patriarch, Douglas, and his wife, Una, while my father became close friends with their son Michael, a rugged, handsome man who looked like a longer-haired Cajun clone of Elvis Presley in his photogenic *Viva Las Vegas* screen-idol era. In the time my father knew him, Michael had three different wives and three children with them; the first wife went on to become a famous cosmetics artist in Hollywood, while the last became a crack addict–turned–born again Baptist. Michael had a reckless streak to put my father's to shame, and for a brief period after my grandfather split up the family business, my father and Michael attempted to run a partnership of their own. Michael would arrive at fur auctions dressed in rabbit-skin vests, leather pants, and alligator boots and try to outbid everyone on everything. My father soon learned how it felt to dissolve a partnership he knew in his heart was never going to work.

Also like my father, Michael had a voracious appetite for drugs, but unlike my father, he had a much greater hunger to consume them intravenously. During the 1990s, Michael contracted hepatitis C and fled from Louisiana to Wyoming, where he died.

My father believed that the only surviving members of the family were Michael's younger sisters, Michele and Daniele. But when we rang the doorbell to their home, we were met by Daniele's seventeen-year-old daughter, Amanda, a little harlequin of a girl dressed in a faded Felix the Cat T-shirt and a pair of military fatigues. She explained that her parents were out grocery shopping and would be back soon. My father told her that he was an old friend of her late uncle Michael's and that once, when Michael was on the verge of being divorced by one of his wives, my father insisted Michael get down on his hands and knees and beg her to take him back. In telling the story, my father made himself cry. Amanda did not invite us into the house.

When Daniele returned home with her husband, Jody, she recognized my father right away. An ample, affable woman, she had vivid memories of the many instances in which her family's history overlapped with ours; just as Adelphia did, she still called my grandfather "Mister Bob." Her house contained the same pool table at which Mister Bob had challenged her father to many a late-night game, and the same couch at which Mister Bob used to fall asleep, a lit cigar dangling from his mouth, until he was woken up by the sting of ash burning a hole in his shirt.

Daniele seemed genuinely delighted by our surprise visit; she told us stories of how my grandfather had taught her to sing "Bei Mir Bist du Schon," and how she had once owned a Siberian husky named Maddy G., a combination of my mother's name and my father's first initial. Then she called up her older sister, Michele, who lived nearby in Thibodaux, to tell her we were here. Michele arrived soon after, a stylish woman in a pant suit and a pair of designer sunglasses atop her head, toting her eleven-year-old daughter, Maddy, and a steel cigarette case proudly stamped with the words TRAILER TRAMP.

At the outset, there was a natural give-and-take to the afternoon's conversation. Michele and Daniele were not oblivious to Michael's drug problem—"his demons," they said—but they had fond recollections of his generosity and charisma and the beautiful, poetic letters he wrote to them that they later discovered were cribbed from Cat Stevens songs. Michele did not shed a single tear as she described seeing her brother for the last time, dying of liver disease and bone cancer in a Cheyenne hospital, too proud to let any of his other family members see him in such a state. "He thought he was invincible," Michele said. "That's how he was to the end."

My father was upbeat as he recounted some of his favorite stories about abusing drugs under Michael's supervision: the time the two of them got high on peyote with my mother and Michael's girlfriend at the time and drove off, stoned, to meet my grandparents for dinner at a nearby seafood restaurant; the time Michael introduced them to animal tranquilizers, which made my mother curl up into a ball and declare erroneously, "You gave me heroin!"

Eventually, my father reverted to his familiar overbearing form. "I'm going to tell you a story," he said with a sense of urgency, "because I've got to tell you as much as I remember." Only, what followed was not a single story but the tangled and messy web of the numerous narrative threads he'd been stitching all week: how his father had split the business with him, thus providing him the motivation to beat his drug problem; how he had fruitlessly counseled Michael to beg forgiveness from his soon-to-be ex-wife; and how he had discovered his father's glass eye but was able to confront him about it only when he was high. Everything he saw or heard provided the trigger for another story or moral lesson—how much he appreciated a good salad; how children who do not grow up around dogs or cats go on to live lives vastly inferior to those who do—and nothing provoked these reminiscences more than the sound of his own reminiscing. While Daniele and Michele listened to him politely, their daughters sat on a nearby couch and watched television, pricking their ears and giggling each time my father raised his voice or said a dirty word. Jody said nothing but eyed the scene warily while walking its perimeter like a prison guard, waiting to take action the moment a captive tried to make a run for the wall.

It wasn't as if these people did not have tales of misfortune to equal or exceed my father's. Months after they lost Michael, their mother, Una, died, and a few months after that, their youngest brother, Douglas Jr., an off-road racing enthusiast with a drug problem of his own, died from injuries he sustained in an ATV accident after spending a week on a respirator. He wasn't even the first member of his family to bear the name Douglas Jr.; he had inherited it from a sibling he never knew, an elder Douglas Jr. who was killed in a car crash on Mardi Gras, the holiest day in the New Orleans calendar, in 1966. Michael had been riding in that same doomed vehicle, but he was thrown clear of the wreckage and only had to spend the next year in a full-body cast.

The Fonsecas were not the only family whose lives were forever altered by that event. This was the accident in which my father lost his kid brother, David. He was the boy who slept in the cot next to my father's in the bedroom they shared with their older sister; the kid who broke his leg when my father encouraged him, too soon, to take the training wheels off his bike, and for whom he used to get down on his knees so they could box at the same height; and the optimistic high school senior who, in the winter of 1966, had just seen his older brother get married and was looking forward to graduating so he could join him and their father in their new business partnership.

On the night of Mardi Gras, David was among a group of young men that included Michael Fonseca and the first Douglas Jr., driving on a two-lane, two-directional highway from a party in Raceland to another party in New Orleans. In attempting to pass a car, their driver had steered into the oncoming lane when the vehicle ahead of them started to accelerate. A second car was headed straight at them in the oncoming lane, and their driver had just enough time to swerve so that they were hit from the side and not head-on. The driver and Michael survived the crash; the other passengers were killed, probably instantly.

My grandfather, who was in New Orleans at the time, was the first to learn of the accident. He then called my father, who was in New York, a newlywed for all of three months and still living with his wife in his parents' home in Bronxville, and instructed him to tell my grandmother what had happened. When my father found her to tell her in person, she was out walking her dog and was momentarily delighted by the unexpected encounter with her son. But when she saw his pained expression and realized he'd been crying, she knew that something horrible had occurred.

For many months my family mourned David's loss; after my grandfather returned home from New Orleans, he locked himself into his dead son's former bedroom and refused to come out. But my father, I am told, took it harder than anyone. Even as my grandparents began to recover from their grief, my father rebuffed their attempts to discuss David's death and would walk—or run—away from them if they so much as mentioned his name.

Yet as soon as he had a child of his own, my father found all of his seemingly intractable positions on the subject willingly and easily reversed. Above the objections of those family members who warned him that the name was cursed, he made the one meaningful stubborn decision that would offset a lifetime's worth of meaningless stubbornness: he named his first son after his dead brother. It would never matter if his brother's possessions and artwork decorated every square inch of his apartment or if they were nowhere to be seen; whether he visited his brother's grave once a day or once every five years. Each time he called out his son's name, he would be reminded of the boy he hoped would one day grow up to be his companion, his confidant, his apprentice, and his friend.

Whether Daniele and Michele were thinking of this incident when my father came to visit, or whether they were simply showing Southern deference to an old man who liked to talk, they let him exhaust his supply of stories before he determined it was time to move along (with some gentle prodding from his chaperone for the day, who was feeling guilty for having inflicted him upon these unsuspecting if hospitable folk). Somehow he even bamboozled them into giving him their email addresses, a move they would soon learn to regret. "I'm going to delude you—not delude you, *deluge* you, with email," he said, and I have no doubt he made good on the promise. Before I left, Michele assured me she'd look me up when she and her daughter visited New York the following month, but I really don't blame her for not following through.

At the Fonsecas' doorstep, my father stopped to retell the story of how my grandfather had split up the family business, and as he sat in the passenger seat of our rental car, he was talking about how he'd coached Michael to reconcile with his wife, and then I started the engine and we were gone.

On our last night in New Orleans, as we sat on our beds at an airport-adjacent hotel, eating fast food we'd picked up at a drive-through window and waiting for *The Sopranos* to come on television, my father was perhaps more excited than at any previous point in the trip. He stood up occasionally to pace the room and wring his hands. What he wanted to do most of all was talk to someone about all the petty fears and trifling secrets that he'd needlessly kept bottled up inside him for so long.

"David," he said, "do you think I could talk to you at some point about my sexual fantasies?"

"Maybe," I said. "Just not right now."

When we boarded our plane back to New York, a tiny two-engine puddle-jumper of a jet, my father's wheeled suitcase proved too large to fit in the overhead compartment. A flight attendant with a mediocre command of the English language asked him to tie a flimsy orange tag to its handle and leave the bag at the door by the front of the plane.

Where could he mean? I thought. *The cabin door through which we entered the plane? The cockpit door? That mysterious auxiliary door in the airport passageway, thirty feet off the ground, that seems to open out to nowhere? In front of the door? Behind the door?* Even if I could not understand this person, my father evidently could, because he took his bag up to the front of the plane, placed it wherever he thought he was supposed to, and came back to his seat.

All I could think for the next three hours and 1,300 miles, more wholeheartedly than any of the anger or frustration or relief I felt at the completion of our journey, was: *Please let him have put his bag in the right place. Please let this man's suitcase be waiting for him when he gets off this plane.* They say there are no atheists in foxholes, and in Row 18 of Continental flight 3056 to Newark Airport, there were none to be found, either.

CHAPTER 10

I had come unstuck in time. It's not a phenomenon that afflicts only famous literary characters, venerated satirists, and survivors of the firebombing of Dresden; regular people can experience it, too. In fact, I believe that each of us is entitled to one entire day that affects us so completely, it immediately reorders the narrative of our lives, declaring itself the crucial chapter in the story that unlocks all the others. The moment becomes the center of our personal universe, and we revolve around it, continuing to live it and relive it long after the action of the day would seem to have been completed. That day for me was my wedding day.

I know it's sort of an obvious, cop-out choice, but that's how profound a day it was for me. You don't have to take my word for it: the power of the occasion was so great that it compelled one friend of mine to propose to his girlfriend on the day he came home from my bachelor party. I was sufficiently excited that I had won a cap gun at an arcade during the trip; he married her three weeks after my own wedding. Two weeks after that, one of my groomsmen proposed to his girlfriend. (She accepted.) That's the kind of impact it had on people who were merely bystanders to the event.

For me, the day lingers around me so completely that sometimes I feel like it is still happening to me; while I am seated at my office computer, my pulse quickens and the hairs on my arms stand at attention because I expect that at any moment, a tuxedo-clad maître d' is going to burst into the room, put me on a golf cart, and send me off to a garden where a bride, a rabbi, and two hundred friends, relatives, acquaintances, and various other Jews in sunglasses await. Right now you are reading these words on a page, and I'm taking my first bite of wedding cake, or listening to my best man recite a Frank O'Hara poem at the wedding reception, or wondering petulantly why I have to visit all the tables of my new wife's relatives and family friends before I can cross the dance floor and congregate with the wedding guests I recognize.

Sometimes I experience different parts of the day simultaneously. I am dancing in my underwear in front of Amy in our bedroom, singing along to "Call Any Vegetable" by Frank Zappa and the Mothers of Invention, hours before we leave for our rehearsal dinner, trying to pretend to myself that I am not the least bit anxious or uncertain about what's soon to happen to us. At the same time, I am being woken up by a bleeping chime on my cellphone on the morning after the wedding, awaking to the fact that Amy and I have slept through the blaring alarm clock we set for ourselves an hour ago, and have only fifteen minutes to shower, dress, and assemble our belongings before a taxi comes to take us to the airport for our honeymoon.

At some point between these two events, I am standing in the middle of a dance floor at a reception hall in the Bronx, dressed in a tuxedo and joined arm in arm with my new bride as we dance a competent hora at a wedding celebration we once vowed would feature no religious traditions or liturgy whatsoever. We are surrounded by two concentric spinning circles of my friends and relatives, and of hers, trying to draw my eyes in every direction at once. There go her mother, father, brother, aunts, and uncles, the cousin who wrote all the hit songs for the J. Geils Band in the 1980s; here come my aunts and uncles, cousins, the old silver-haired women from the bungalow colonies with their glossy animal-print tops and pointy fingernails till tomorrow, my sister, and my mother.

"Where's Dad?" I ask my mother in a moment when our two circles briefly align.

All I hear her say is "You know your father" before the momentum of the dance whisks her away.

I have time to contemplate this briefly: *Do I?* Did I gain enough insight into him to say why he's not here at this exact instant? Is it enough to know that he sends his regards from his table at the outer perimeter of the banquet hall, where, in a few minutes, someone will accidentally set a napkin on fire, and where he is probably caught up in some compelling (to him) conversation while he shouts passionately into a confederate's ear, or too shy, still, to join us in our clumsy choreography?

The circles of dancers widen their gyrations, then they close in around me and they take me to pieces.

Now I'm somewhere else entirely, floating in a metal cabin forty thousand feet above the earth, with nothing to distract me except blue sky above, blue water below, a nine-hundred-page Neal

Stephenson novel in my lap, and a passable Michel Gondry movie on a screen in front of me. Amy and I are on our way to paradise, feeling like we just got away with robbing a bank. We are armed with a stack of the most diplomatic and obsequiously worded documents from her father, a former airline pilot, politely pleading to their intended recipients that their bearers please be upgraded to first class from coach because, even though you are a big, faceless airline company unaccustomed to acts of kindness and generosity, and paid minimal attention to their author during all the years he flew your airplanes and never collided with any landmark New York skyscrapers, this is his daughter and her new husband, and they are on their honeymoon. The letters prove unnecessary when a friend of Amy's, still employed by this same airline, bumps us up to first-class seats without our asking. I got choked up a few times on my wedding day, but when this friend told us we wouldn't have to spend a six-hour flight from Dallas–Fort Worth to Maui sitting in coach, I cried.

In a few hours, Amy and I will be inducted into a weeklong nonstop Polynesian minstrel show whose participants have been taught to interject the word *mahalo*, Hawaiian for "thank you," at every possible opportunity. The garbage bins at the fast-food restaurants will say *mahalo* on their lids, and the bathrooms will have placards that say MAHALO FOR NOT SMOKING and MAHALO FOR WASHING YOUR HANDS. Until then we are overwhelmed by the simple amenities of hot washcloths and on-demand servings of alcohol and hot-fudge sundaes, and we have been pampered into a state of catatonic honesty and openness. Under the influence of ice cream and recirculated air, she makes her first confession to me as my wife.

"I didn't want to say anything until the day was over and we were safely in the air," she says, "but I was scared that something was going to happen with your dad."

"What do you mean?" I ask.

"I was afraid that he was going to . . . get high. You know, *at the wedding*."

Now, a hermetically sealed capsule suspended thousands of feet above the ground and hours away from the nearest landmass may not be the ideal location to pick a fight with a woman who has been your wife under twenty-four hours. So all I say to her in response is "Come on, you didn't really think that was going to happen, did you?"

But what I'm really thinking is: *Are you fucking kidding me? Do you sincerely think that my father's top priority on the day that his firstborn and (I would like to believe) most beloved child gets married is to score cocaine and snort it up before he walks me down the aisle? Do you imagine that this agenda item appears anywhere on his list of things to do for the day? Do you know so little about this man, and have his quietly heroic efforts in the name of sobriety done nothing to convince you that he is capable of keeping his addiction in check—if not for the last five years, then at least on the one day that means more than anything to his son?*

And then I think: *Hold on a second—this woman does not really know my father personally. She wasn't raised by him, didn't grow up alongside him. What she thinks she knows is what I've told her about him—the depiction of him that I've presented to her, that she is attempting to defend me from in advance, for an offense he hasn't yet committed. If her impressions of him are based on faulty information, where is she getting her information? If she can't understand my father in the way that I want him to be understood, whose fault is that, really?*

And then I think: *Just a minute, you goddamned hypocrite. How*

*can you, in your mind, right now, ask for clemency for your father
when you yourself have sentenced him to imaginary deaths over and
over again for the very same crime—the crime of being who he used to
be? If you can't admit to yourself, and mean it, that he's not that person anymore, why should anyone else believe it? What makes you so
special that you can hold it over his head forever? Don't you think he
understands that last bit of presumptive innocence went up his nose a
long time ago? Don't you think he bears this on his back every day, and
if he can carry this around for thirty years, doesn't that put the guy who
spent three measly days up on the cross—whom we don't believe in, by
the way—to shame?*

No part of me has any time to answer these questions. The farther our plane travels and the closer we get to our blissful arrival,
the more I feel like something is coming apart—the harder the
plane seems to be tugging on some sort of safety net, and the
faster it feels like it's unraveling from underneath me. A delicate
web in which I always knew my place is coming apart strand by
strand, and soon I won't have any framework to exist in at all. I'll
just end up drifting in empty space, like the plane currently carrying me, with no origin and no destination. A hole is opening up
in the fabric of my familiar world, and I dive in headfirst.

Now I am somewhere earlier in time, in the days before the wedding. I haven't yet celebrated my wedding eve by smoking pot and
eating bagels with my best man in a townhouse in Brooklyn
Heights. I haven't yet endured the following morning, fixated on
the distant—yet feasible!—possibility that our rabbi will miss the
last train that could get him to the wedding on time, and the lone
person without whom the ceremony literally cannot be performed will be devastatingly late or perhaps fail to show at all.

And I haven't yet spent an afternoon riding in a chauffered van to my own nuptials, wondering for the sake of argument what would happen if, at the next red light, I simply opened a door and ran to the horizon.

I am about to have my last telephone conversation with my father before the date in question. We've been speaking more frequently lately, for practical purposes. Two telephone calls ago, the exchange went like this:

"You know, Dad, it's customary for the father of the groom to give a speech at the rehearsal dinner."

"Shit. It is? Can you write it for me?"

"I don't know about that. I can *help* you write it. I could try to help you think of things to say."

"What should I talk about?"

"Probably a memory of me. Or of us. You could tell a story from when I was younger that shows how I've changed from then to now. Or a story that shows how I'm still basically the same. That's what I'd do, anyway."

"What if I can't come up with anything?"

"You'll think of something. Why don't you take a few days and try to come up with some memories? I know you know how to do that."

"What if it upsets you or embarrasses you?"

"I wouldn't worry about that. If you say sincerely whatever's in your heart, I'm sure it will be fine."

"Hey, just because you can easily imagine it doesn't mean it's easy for everyone to do."

One telephone call ago, the exchange went like this:

"So how is the speech coming?"

"I think I came up with a memory, but I don't know if it's one I should tell or not."

"Well, why don't you tell it to me, and then I can decide."

"Okay. Do you remember when I was teaching you how to drive, and you ran that red light that time, and I said, 'Hey, what are you thinking?' And you said, 'I'm thinking about pussy'?"

". . . Don't tell that story."

The last phone call almost doesn't happen at all; I start by calling my mother to beg her to please be on time—no, as early as possible—to the venue on the day of the wedding.

"I'm probably going to get there first thing in the morning to get my makeup done," she says. "But you know your father. He wants to take separate cars."

"Don't let him do it, Mom," I say. *"Don't."*

"You can tell him yourself," she says.

". . ."

"Hiya, Davey."

"Hi, Dad."

"Howya doin'?"

"Counting down. You?"

"Still livin'."

"You guys going to be there on Sunday?"

"Of course we're going to be there. You think we'd miss it?"

"What time are you planning to get there?"

"Well, if it were up to me, I'd leave whenever I had to. But you know your mother—she's got to get there early so she can have her face made up and put on her dress. I was thinking I might take my own car so I can—"

"*Please* don't, Dad. *Please.* Can you just this once ride in with her? I know it means you'll have to get up earlier, but—"

"Okay, Davey," he says with mock oppression, to let me know he's not really oppressed and to remind me that, yes, in fact, he sort of is.

"How you feelin'?" he asks. "You nervous? It's okay to be nervous, you know." This is his way of telling me that not only is it permissible to be nervous, but it is his preference that I be nervous—that the only way he can think to respond to an uncertain situation is to get nervous, and therefore, he cannot understand why anyone else placed in the same situation would not also get nervous. Thus he would be deeply suspicious if I were anything but nervous.

So I give him a taste of what he wants. "Okay, yeah, I'm a little nervous," I say. "There's just so many moving pieces that have to come together, it seems impossible that they're all going to fall into place the way we've planned. One or two, you'd think, would have to go wrong. But am I worried that I don't have the nerve to go through with it? Nah."

"You mean you're not going to get up early in the morning and go fishing?" he says with a chuckle. This is a reference to a true story—this is how he spent the morning of his own wedding: by himself on a fishing boat, utterly unaware of how much time had elapsed or when he was due at his ceremony, until his future wife and in-laws went to the lake where he was happily not getting married and escorted him to the service.

"Not me," I say. "I just hope Amy makes it there, too."

"Don't you worry," my father says with uncharacteristic certainty. "She'll be there."

"So how's the speech coming?"

"Pretty good," he says. "I think I've got a good story this time. It's about Mommy and me and how you and Amy remind me of us. She's been real good for you, David. I think she's been good for you in a lot of ways."

"Yeah?" I say. "How?"

"She's evened you out," he says. "She's calmed you down."

There is a lot bound up in such a short remark. It implies, first of all, that I am or once was someone in need of calming down but also someone capable of calming down—that in my father's eyes, I could still be that irritable, angry, tightly wound person I didn't want to be perceived as, and that he was at last able to see me as something other than that person fixed in his mind for most of my adult life.

It implies something else, too: in order for my father to have any sense of before and after, it means that he has to be paying attention. Here I was, all this time, thinking of myself like some kind of anthropologist conducting a field study, taking notes and recording my thoughts from a safe, objective distance, and never once did it occur to me, what if, from behind the bars of his cage, my subject were performing the same experiment on me? Talk about your fundamental attribution error. He who fights with his parents should be careful lest he thereby become a parent. And if you gaze long into your father, does your father not gaze back?

This is as close as I will get to a pep talk from my father before the wedding. I will receive no affirmation from him that on this day, in his eyes, I've finally become a man, no fumbling, clinical explanation of what I'm supposed to do on my wedding night. I have known for some time that one of his fondest desires was to see his son find a companion for life, and I trust that seeing that wish fulfilled must bring him some quantity of joy. But does the absence of having any more dreams for his son—indeed, the impending absence of having a son at all—fill him with any melancholy?

I must be on to something here, because for once, I am not forced to jump around in time, and events continue to occur in a linear sequence. I go to sleep at night, wake up the next morning in the same bed. I entertain Amy in my underwear, we work on our speeches for that night's rehearsal dinner, and somehow we have confidence that even though it is utterly storming outside— for a moment I wish old Adelphia were here from New Orleans to remind me that, indeed, these things do pass—we have checked enough weather websites on the Internet to assure ourselves that tomorrow will be as clear and sunny as any day we'll soon see in Hawaii. Compared to some of the other leaps of faith we are about to take, that one seems pretty trivial. Still, I can't resist screaming a hearty "Fuck off!" to the two women who try to steal the cab we have narrowly hailed in the pouring rain, because it helps to break the tension.

The rehearsal dinner turns out to be the largest gathering of people I am related to or otherwise intimately acquainted with since my bar mitzvah, and the first time in as long since I am the center of that many people's attention, which of course is bizarre and unsettling. It's as if the world has somehow shrunk to a small enough point that you are the closest thing to a celebrity that remains in it. Everyone is grateful for the feeling of rejuvenation and potential for rebirth that you bring to the room, because they could use it—they have no more joyous transitions to look forward to in their own lives.

There is my uncle, my mother's brother, whom, the last time I saw him regularly, I called "Uncle Pussycat" for the short prickly mustache he had begun to grow; now he's got a full white beard, and he's old enough that no one can chastise him for attending tonight's festivities in a Hawaiian shirt (authentic, purchased in Maui, as it happens). There is an old friend of my father's from our bungalow-colony summers, who used to be strong enough, when I used to be small enough, to lift me up out of a pool and hurl me to its opposite end; now he looks like his spine can barely support his saggy weight, and his eyeballs can hardly support their droopy lids. What happened to these people? Didn't they once seem like gods, immortal, eternally youthful? Don't tell me they expect me, a kid, and my child bride, to pick up where they left off. And don't tell me they once thought about themselves what I think now: that this is never going to happen to me, that I'm never going to get old like they did and like they saw their parents do. They only thought they could prevent it from happening to themselves, but me, I know it. I can *will* it to be so.

It is after all fifty or sixty of us sit down to eat and our salads are served that things really begin to get interesting. One by one, we go around the room giving speeches—some prepared, some extemporaneous, and some prepared to look extemporaneous—that are testimonials to my character or Amy's greatness or the institution of marriage itself. Never have I been in such a room, where so many people want me to look optimistically toward my future and are actually on the verge of convincing me to do so.

Each of my groomsmen and Amy's bridesmaids share a miniature observation from which they extrapolate that we are perfect for each other and will remain together for time immemorial. My mother gives a speech in which she quotes George Sand— *George Sand!* A sixty-three-year-old woman from the Bronx with a high school education, who still occasionally mixes up Billy Idol and Billy Ocean, quoting *George Sand!*—reminding us all that "there is only one happiness in life, to love and be loved," before she gets choked up and can barely finish.

Then Amy and I give our speeches, and quite frankly, we kill. Hers is a little more theatrical, mine a little more artless, but by coincidence, we have both chosen to tell the story of the same moment: a dinner we shared, about two years before this day, when she told me that she couldn't imagine herself being married to anyone. Her account tells of how she got over that attitude, while mine tells of how I bided my time while she got over that attitude, but in the end, at least, we came to the same place. I could recite in more specific detail how great these speeches were, but then I'd just be bragging.

There's one person who hasn't been accounted for. My father is visibly nervous as he stands up from his seat, shivering in place and wringing his hands, as if he's fallen out of a boat and is trying to rinse out all the water he soaked up. "Okay," he announces, "here we go." Then his voice doubles in volume: "Into the valley of death rode the six hundred!" he shouts, extending a fist, accompanied by a sound effect from his mouth that to his ears perhaps resembles the Russian cannonade at the Battle of Balaclava. "No, wait—" he says. "What am I saying?" This is how he behaves when there is no pressure on him and absolutely nothing is at stake.

Finally, he settles down and tells a quick story of the day he introduced his future wife to his father and how it reminds him of the day I introduced him to Amy. I'm not sure if everyone in the room can hear him, because he's talking so rapidly, but I think it's a pretty good effort, especially given how much difficulty he had in coming up with something to say.

Later, when all the speeches are over and the guests are mingling from table to table, I discover at my father's seat his secret weapon: a cheat sheet—a piece of shirt cardboard, probably taken from a dress shirt he opened that very morning, or will perhaps wear tomorrow, on which the entire text of his speech has already been written down. In my mother's handwriting.

Here is how my father's rehearsal dinner speech reads, in its entirety:

Hi Everyone—
    I'm Gerry ~~Dad's~~ David's Dad.

And I wanted to make a toast to Amy + David—

When David's Mom (Maddy) & I were dating—I brought her to meet my parents—and within minutes of meeting her, my Dad said "you have my permission to marry her." ~~In those days~~ When he said it, I'm sure I was embarrassed—But today I real-ize what my dad saw in me what have seen in David—

Happiness!—

That twinkle in his eye, that board [sic] face smile.

So at this time let me wish you both a long life, a life filled with Happiness.

"And That's All Folks."

I would wager that those 107 words took hours to compose and that each one of them was pondered, pored over, contemplated and recontemplated, and then vetted by my mother before they were ever committed to that piece of cardboard—an artifact I save and plan to venerate as if it were the envelope on which Lincoln composed the Gettysburg Address. In the history of my father's life, it is a document as valuable and as rare: the record of the first time he was asked to commit his words to any enduring medium, to think about what each one meant before he or his wife wrote it down. Under that kind of pressure, he struggled with every single one, just like . . . well—like me.

We were not so different in this respect. Perhaps all along, we had both been engaged in the same project without realizing it. We both endeavored to preserve all the pieces of our family his-tory that were meaningful to us, the ones we thought were certain to be eradicated by time and neglect if no one else made the effort to enshrine them somewhere. We were each the self-appointed family historian of our generation—we just worked in different mediums. If it took a certain amount of focus and frustration for me to get my words down on a page, for my father, the same act could not be accomplished without an agony that he found utterly unbearable. It was easier for him to live his life surrounded by a thin mist of nostalgia. If he ever stopped reciting and re-reciting his beloved stories, he ran the risk of even greater agony, that they would disappear forever. All he could do to forestall this was to tell them, and tell them, and tell them again.

Was I getting any closer to the lesson that the constant repetition and rerouting of my wedding events was supposed to teach me? I was gone again, off to another destination in time, before I found out.

Amy and I are a week into our honeymoon. In four days we have succeeded in driving on just about every road in Maui and seen just about every feature, including the improbable sight of Charles Lindbergh's grave: a wide slab covered in rocks and marked by a fading, rusted plaque in a mostly empty field behind a tiny, unremarkable church. In this time we have enjoyed so many different activities, variously so mundane and so perverse that I won't dare describe them here, and our only regret is that so far only one person has attempted to sell us weed. (That he did so on the steps of a courthouse only made it seem that much more suspicious.)

Everywhere we go, we meet other young couples on their honeymoons, who seem like us but not quite—like photocopies that came out smudged or crumpled or elongated. Sure, they seem happy and blissful, but are they truly fulfilled? Do they desperately need each other? Would they spend their lazy weekends together singing Stephen Sondheim songs at the living room piano, and would they stay up all night convincing each other that they aren't fat or friendless, and would they plunge the toilet without complaint when the other one clogs it up? I don't think so, but then they probably don't think so about us, either.

For our penultimate dinner, we have chosen to travel from our luxury hotel complex in one resort town to another luxury hotel complex in another nearby resort town. We stand on the beach with the other honeymooners, waiting until right before sunset, when we turn our attention to a set of nearby cliffs. We have been waiting to watch a Hawaiian native perform a cliff dive. I expect a grand act of showmanship—swelling music, a defiant full-speed charge toward the precipice, an acrobatic display on the way down, concluded with a mighty splash. But no announcement is made when the diver appears on the cliff; he walks to the edge and jumps in, landing with a quiet, whispering *plunk*. We see him later in the dining room while we eat our buffet dinners, walking from table to table, educating patrons on a plastic fish he is carrying around. Everything here is the slightest bit inauthentic.

I am toughing my way through my third or fourth piece of prime rib, and Amy and I are reciting a familiar conversation about how we're not going to have children for at least a few years. "They say it changes everything," she says. "I don't want to do it until I feel like I've worked and I've lived and done everything else I want to do."

"Yeah," I say, "assuming we have a choice in the matter."

What I mean by this is: *Am I the only person at this table who feels like his life is coming apart at the seams, like it's being pulled upon from every direction until it bursts? Can't you feel it, too? Doesn't it scare you to death, back to life, and to death again to think about what we've done? Everything we could say for certain about our lives is over. Our security is gone. Now we're no one else's responsibility. Now we're no one else's obligation. Everything that happens to us, from this moment on, is our own fault.*

Then she takes my hand, and without realizing it, she solves the riddle and banishes all doubt with her reply. "We're our own family now," she says.

What she means, or what I decide she means, is that we are all potentialities at any given time, but our potential will never be greater than it is in this moment. It was this transcendental quality that attracted our guests to our rehearsal dinner, that they were celebrating at our wedding. We savored the sensation of that energy, too, but now we have to start expending it. From every day forward, we will become less nebulous and more defined, but if we're smart enough to see it happening, and careful enough to pay attention, we can choose this definition for ourselves and be the ones shaping it, rather than letting our circumstances do it for us. We are now a unit so tight, with a membership so exclusive that not even our parents can force themselves into it—although we can allow them in if we so choose.

What kind of couple will we be? Will we be socialites with a large circle of casual acquaintances, or homebodies who count each other as our only friends? Will we be coldly unapproachable or unbearably cute? Will we be nose-to-the-grindstone strivers or coulda-been, if-only-I'd, the-world's-against-me failures? Will it all fall apart in five years over some factor we never could have anticipated? Will we become swingers, drive cross-country on a whim, or live in a yurt? Will we have pets? All the answers reside in us somewhere, in parts of ourselves we cannot tap in to yet, and that give us unmatched greatness.

There is just one more stop left on this history tour that I need to see, and now the destination is obvious to me. I am standing outside the entrance to a garden, sweating pleasantly in the first tuxedo I have ever owned, while from inside a musical quartet strikes up a string arrangement of Joy Division's "Love Will Tear Us Apart." Two men pull back the latticed garden doors to reveal, dreamlike, all my friends and relatives present and future. The sun is so high in the sky that they are all using their paper programs as fans and visors, and they stare at me like I'm an alien, or maybe they are aliens who have never seen a human.

Before I can enter, my parents approach from either side to escort me to the altar. Holding my mother's hand is like grasping a cloud; we make the slightest of contact and she glides effortlessly down the aisle as if the whole day is a pageant for her. My father clutches my other arm with the subtlety of a steel bear trap; he stumbles with every few steps we take, never quite able to anticipate our pace, and drives his shoulder into mine as if he has forgotten that he and I are not quite the same width. We reach the end of the aisle and I kiss my mother, and then, in front of everyone whose opinion matters to me, what the heck, I kiss my father, too.

And then—well, you know what happens at weddings. Amy enters with her parents, and the aliens watch her progress to the altar. The rabbi recites his liturgy, removing, as requested, any reference to God or the laws of Moses; Amy's brother reads a Shakespearean sonnet (her selection, classy and delicate) and my best man reads a passage from Fitzgerald's *This Side of Paradise* (my choice, ironic and ominous); a tiny bug flies unseen into the ear of our rabbi. We are married.

Only here is how the ceremony ends. In the same moment that I reach my arms around my new wife and kiss her for the first time—and I do not learn this until later, because in the moment I am otherwise occupied—my father leans in to my mother and gives her a sweet and unself-conscious kiss. It is an endearing if slightly strange moment to see captured in a photograph, which is how I saw it for the first time: you don't know where to look, and when you realize you're being allowed to peer into two highly personal and intimate moments, it's almost easier to focus on Amy's bouquet, or the big white lifeless column standing stolidly in between the two couples.

Some former, backward-looking version of me might have been angry or embarrassed that my father, in a typically oblivious, Dad-like way, had co-opted what was supposed to be my moment. But aside from the check for five thousand dollars that he would press into my jacket pocket a few hours later, I can't think of a more useful gift he could have given me to begin my new life. For all his years of trying to illuminate the eerie, inescapable parallels between our lives, sometimes inadvertently creating those correspondences in the process, he had proved his point with one indelible image. If at this moment I was pure, limitless potentiality, he was the resolution of it—one possible but hardly inevitable terminus on the pathway. Here I was at roughly the same age as my father when he made all the terrible choices that would pit him against his family for the next three decades. For all the love and hatred, passion and anger, that I had shown him, these feelings meant nothing if I could not surpass him in the circumstances where he had fallen short, and if I could not at least match him in the areas where he had succeeded.

What guaranteed that one of my many habits and vices would not fester over the months and years to become a debilitating, soul-sucking affliction? Nothing. How did I know that, amplified, magnified, and repeated over time, my addiction to videogames, my excessive masturbation, my temper, or that weird relentlessness I get sometimes wouldn't do me in? I didn't. Where was it certified that the newborn who would someday sit atop my shoulders, with the same look of bewilderment I wore when I sat atop my father's, would not grow up to resent me for reasons I can only begin to imagine? No place. Who could say for certain that, even if I did everything right that my father did wrong, I would still turn out to be a decent husband or parent? Nobody. How much more did I know now than when my father undertook these same responsibilities? Zero. Where could I look to find the accumulated wisdom of the past generations of fathers and husbands, that mapped out what to do in any moment of uncertainty and made every mistake of the past utterly preventable in the future? Nowhere.

Who could decide whether the last thirty-two years of my life would be allowed to dictate the course of the thirty-two to come? Me. When would I know for certain that I had lived up to the challenge that my father's life presented, and fulfilled the potential that this day offered?

The only answer I can supply is the motto my father spoke to me so many times before, the watchword of the prideful Jewish parent: *When you have children of your own, then you'll know.*

Those are the words that break the spell, that lift the curse, that end the recursion and allow time to move forward. A guy and a girl get married, a DJ plays, somebody drinks too much, somebody has the steak, and somebody else has the fish. Onward.

On a winter's day, I returned to my parents' home in Monticello. A recent cold snap had created gleaming icicles that dangled perilously from power lines and forced the trees to bow reverently as a bus drove me past them. For a town whose main attractions were a Wal-Mart and a racetrack with electronic slot machines, it was as austere and sanctified as I'd ever see it. The house, however, was disheveled, with clothes piled on top of couches, blood pressure machines piled on top of calculators, boots piled on top of beach towels on top of firewood. My father was still immersed in his nostalgia-preserving computer, though he was also excited about his new iPhone, as well as a recently purchased GPS, which I thought was especially silly. "When do you ever go anywhere that you don't know where you are?" I asked.

"Yeah," he said, "but I can use it, like, to find drugs. I just type in 'drugs,' and it takes me right to them." Everybody laughed at that.

What I had hoped for on this trip was to see my father swimming, engaged in the activity that had been responsible for his remarkable weight loss of recent years. We were not an athletic family, because athleticism meant control—control over yourself and over your body. It meant your will was more powerful than all the combined forces conspiring to do the opposite of what you wanted.

But I needed to take only one look at him to realize there wouldn't be any swimming today. He had gained back most of the weight and then some; his belly had reacquired its familiar round shape, and he had added a pair of suspenders to his wardrobe. Plus, he said, he had a case of indigestion "to beat the band." Seeking medical advice, he had called my sister, who told him that using over-the-counter remedies was a waste of time. "Yeah," he had told her, "but consider the alternative." It's no use, she said, and he answered with a favorite personal maxim that meant roughly the same thing: "Nothing means nothing."

I did not come away empty-handed from the visit. My parents and I were having lunch in a diner, where I was recounting for them the family-appropriate exploits of my honeymoon, when my mother shared a story I had never heard. In the early days of their marriage, she and my father had traveled to Mexico, where they booked an afternoon fishing trip on a sailboat and were likely the only non-native, English-speaking Caucasians on the ship. When they were many miles from land, the sky was overtaken by a terrible storm that threatened to sweep the ship out to the ocean or wreck it completely. The coast was so far away that there was no time to get back before the storm hit, so the only option was to drop anchor and ride it out. But as the crew rapidly searched the ship, they discovered they had left the anchor behind, if they ever had one. The storm loomed closer.

My mother, by her own telling, was panicked and useless. The resigned crew, as best as she could understand, was making peace with God. But my father somehow kept his calm. He summoned his shipmates and got them to gather all the chairs on board, tie them together with a length of rope, and secure the loose end of that rope to the ship before they threw the chairs overboard. The boat was now moored. When the storm came through, it took away my mother's desire to return to Mexico any time soon, but it left the ship and its passengers intact.

I thought about this story incessantly on my journey home, one more bus ride along that charmed route that was precisely a hundred miles, two hours, and two *New York Times* crossword puzzles in duration. How could I have gone my entire life without ever hearing this tale? When being provided with just one example of my father acting heroically would have been enough to offset all the instances in which he had behaved otherwise, how had some cruel cartel of fate, chance, memory, and my mother conspired to keep it from me?

That, at least, was my old, linear way of looking at events. But if I saw them from another perspective, in the order I had experienced them—in the order that was most convenient and comfortable for me to place them—this decisive and selfless in-carnation of my father was the most current version of him that I knew. In the chronological sequence of his life, it had oc-curred over thirty-five years ago, but to me, he might as well have walked in from the sea, his hair tousled by the wind and rain, a souvenir length of rope across his shoulders. If he could do it even once before, who could say that this bravery was not some innate quality of his? Who could say it would never show up again?

What else could I change about his life and how I thought about him if I just reorganized the order in which I once believed events occurred? How much more of my own life could I validate if I just reshuffled the parts of his that most troubled me—if I tied them to the end of a rope and tossed them overboard like a bunch of tattered deck chairs? Then I could let go of the drug abuse, the prolonged absences, the uncertainty, and the anger. I could cast aside the shame and the secrecy, all the hurt accidentally in-flicted upon me without thinking and without malice. I could say to myself that, as of now, I regret nothing—and accept, as my father had spent all those years telling me, that nothing means *nothing*.

Not only could I do all of that, I could allow myself to admit that I was satisfied with how everything, *everything*, had turned out. I was happy for the loneliness that had shown me never to fear solitude and taught me the value of companionship. I was grateful for the anxiety that never permitted me to be satisfied with mea-ger accomplishments and allowed me to make productive use of sleepless nights. I enjoyed the fights that had instilled in me the ability to construct arguments on a moment's notice and think on my feet, and had demonstrated for me the application of power and the injustice of power applied selfishly. Now I had some power, too. My father had given me life, but I could give life back to him.

I stepped off the bus and back into the wider world. In my own private way, I told my father that he could go on living, because I intended to do the same.

ACKNOWLEDGMENTS

There's an old saying that victory has one hundred fathers, and this book has many parents, natural and otherwise, to thank for its publication, too. It would not exist without Lauren Kern and Adam Moss, in whose pages at *New York* it was first conceived. It would have grown up all wrong without Nina Collins and Bruce Tracy, who taught it to walk and talk and sent it off to school. And it would never have matured without Ryan Doherty, Jill Schwartzman, and Daniel Greenberg, who guided it through some reckless phases with the perfect balance of discipline, attentiveness, and forgiveness.

I could not have come this far without my loving and supportive family, or without Amy, who makes me want to be a father and glad I am not one yet.

ABOUT THE AUTHOR

DAVE ITZKOFF is a reporter on the culture
desk of *The New York Times* and the lead con-
tributor to its popular ArtsBeat blog. He is
the author of *Lads* and has written for numerous publications, including *GQ, Vanity
Fair, Details, Wired, Elle, Spin, The New York
Times Book Review,* and *New York* magazine,
which published the essay from which this
book is adapted. He now has a great relationship with his father.

ABOUT THE TYPE

The text of this book was set in Filosofia. It was designed in 1996 by Zuzana Licko, who created it for digital typesetting as an interpretation of the sixteenth-century typeface Bodoni. Filosofia, an example of Licko unusual font designs, has classical proportions with a strong vertical feeling, softened by rounded droplike serifs. She has designed many typefaces and is the cofounder of *Emigre* magazine, where many of them first appeared. Born in Bratislava, Czechoslovakia, Licko came to the United States in 1986. She studied graphic communications at the University of California at Berkeley, graduating in 1984.